Mountain Biking UK

THE COMPLETE MOUNTAIN BIKE BOOK

Mountain Biking UK

THE COMPLETE MOUNTAIN BIKE BOOK

EDITED BY

TYM MANLEY

First published in 1995 by

Future Books

A division of Future Publishing Limited

30 Monmouth Street, Bath BA1 2BW

Designed by Maria Bowers

Text by Tym Manley, Brant Richards, Derek Purdy, Justin Loretz, Jason McRoy and Paul Smith

Edited by Tass Whitby

Photography by Stockfile:Steve Behr/Nigel Jackson/Dave Stewart,

Jim McRoy/Sportraits, Derek Purdy, Robert Smith Photography, Allsport, Rob Scott

With thanks to PORC (Penshurst Off-Road Circuit)

A CIP catalogue record of this book is

available from the British Library

ISBN: 1 85981 0411

Reprographics by Quadcolour Ltd., Warley, West Midlands

Printed and bound by BPC Paulton Books Ltd.

A member of the British Printing Company

2 4 6 8 10 9 7 5 3 1

Other cycling titles by Future Books:

Grime Time

Masterclass Riding Techniques

Classic Mountain Bike Trails

Wheelwright's Route Guides:

      The Wessex Way

      The Lakeland Loop

      The Coast-to-Coast

      The High Peak Trail

      Trails in Scotland

All the above titles are available from:

The Publisher, Future Books, 30 Monmouth Street, Bath BA1 2BW

Dedication

This book is dedicated to the memory of Jason McRoy who died in a motorcycle accident on 24th August 1995.

Jason's contribution to the book and to *MBUK* magazine, by way of words, pictures and sheer inspiration was huge, as it was to British mountain biking. He was not only Britain's best downhill rider, but the embodiment of everything a mountain bike hero should be – immensely courageous and skilful, but never taking it too seriously, simply revelling in the sheer enjoyment of riding off road and downhill in particular.

Jason was a part of *MBUK*. He was our friend and, through the magazine, he became the friend of all our readers.

We will miss him too completely for words to say. The only consolation we have is that Jason McRoy really lived and enjoyed every minute of his life, doing what he loved doing best – riding his mountain bike.

Contents

C H A P T E R 1

freedom
&excitement

THE SPIRIT OF THE THING, WHAT

A BIKE CAN

DO FOR YOU, HOW IT ALL BEGAN

Tym Manley is the editor of MBUK and MTB Pro. Universally acknowledged as the greatest journalist in his field, mainly because he's the only journalist currently living in a field.
Against all the odds, riding a bike across the sort of terrain you shouldn't be able to has caught the imagination of millions world wide. Mountain biking is more than a sport or a recreation, it has become a statement, encapsulating all the things this growing raft of riders think really important.

This book will try to explain why that is.

We aim to help you get into mountain biking, and the first thing you should know is that it's every bit as likely that mountain biking will get into you.

It's a powerful drug

I don't know what attracted you to this particular form of madness, there are so many entry points that it can catch almost anybody. You might want to get fit, or fancy the adrenalin rush on a full out downhill; you may love the countryside and want to see more of it, or you may want to do amazing jumps; you could be looking forward to the competitive buzz of racing (formally or not) or be planning to ride around the world. Whatever the attraction, it's a grand's worth of trick bits to a slap in the eye with a lump of wet cowpat that you don't know half the pleasure mountain biking has in store for you.

No matter what your age, the depth of your pocket or, within sensible limits, your fitness.

No doubt about it, mountain biking can change your life (and infinitely for the better), but there are a lot of riders who will go further and insist (only half tongue in cheek), that it is, actually, er, the meaning of life.

Claiming that riding bikes in the mud is the meaning of life might look a bit silly, put like that in cold type without the usual accompanying embarrassed grin, but there's no getting away from the fact that there is a strong philosophical, even spiritual, element surrounding mountain biking

If you want the freedom of the hills, mountain bikes are the way to it. They find the buzz in you and it comes out jumping for joy.

Henry Ford's Model T knocked the bicycle for six as a status symbol in the twenties, but in the nineties the MTB is the way to beat the gridlock.

– balanced nicely by a ferocious appetite for tea, buns, beer and, er, gender.

Don't worry, we're not talking religion in any narrow sense here. All mountain biking does is get you fit, drive out life's tensions, relax your mind and then dump you, feeling about as well as you possibly can feel, in the middle of nature's most inspiring unspoilt hills.

And if you don't get some sort of buzz out of that, then you're probably dead. Mountain bikes don't do it to you, but if it's in you they find it.

Remember the old poem about human nature that goes:
'Two men looked through the prison bars,
One saw mud, the other saw stars'?
Well mountain biking gives you the best of both worlds. Fall off in a classic tumbling rinse cycle slamdunk and you'll see stars/mud/stars/mud/stars (in that order).

Sorry, I just stopped being serious about mountain biking being the meaning of life (no one can keep it up for long) and it doesn't have to be that way, but if you become a mountain biker you will become part of a strong, international, group camaraderie based on the understanding that mountain bikers know something other people don't. It may not be true, but it's an excellent feeling.

Cycling re-cycled

The feeling of freedom and excitement which the mountain bike brings with it is, partly at least, a re-flowering of a much older tradition. From the moment the safety bicycle was invented, cycling has given the less than wealthy a sense of freedom and adventure (although the excitement was a lot closer to fear in the day of the Ordinary, what we all call the penny farthing.

It gave anyone who could afford a bike licence to range into the countryside under their own steam, where they liked, at their own pace and in their own time. Women, particularly, found it a liberating machine.

In the twenties and thirties, large groups of young people would go out together, carrying picnics, wearing tweeds and talking about socialism and the latest play of Mr Bernard Shaw.

The thing that put a stop to that little spurt of freedom was Henry Ford's tin box – the cheap motor car. It not only knocked the bike for six as a status symbol, but knocked 'em for six on the highway.

Riding a bike on the roads became a cowering, shrinking sort of business. Forced into the gutter, gooshed with filthy fumes, it lost in freedom what it gained in excitement.

The great majority of people simply stopped cycling.

From the perspective of the urban nineties, it's hard to imagine road cycling ever being a popular and relaxing family activity. But get on a mountain bike, at the start of a long empty stretch of bridleway which snakes off between the secretive hills, and it all comes back.

Without the car, cycling is freedom. Mountain biking is cycling without cars. And more...

The mountain bike has a designed-in potential for excitement greater than any bicycle ever made. It's the key to a vast range of different activities which appeal to an equally wide range of free spirits, from the death-defying stunt king to the stealthy nature lover.

Racing is only one aspect of mountain biking, and if the joy of falling off in front of lots of spectators isn't your thing, that's OK. Go ride the hills.

BICYCLES WITH ATTITUDE

What's the secret of the mountain bike's popularity? Simple. It has something to offer everyone who's into freedom, excitement and fun...

Pan's People

The desire to get out into the countryside and take in the peace and beauty of nature is strong in most mountain bikers. The bike is as quiet and low impact as walking, but allows you to get so much further away from it all in the limited free time most of us have. You can do a weekend's walking in an afternoon, or a week's hike in a weekend.

It's hard work, requiring plenty of self-control and discipline, which is why other countryside users have found that anyone who gets very far off the road on a bike is every bit as civilised as they are.

The twonks, whether on wheels or on foot, never get far from the car park. By the way, mountain bikes, properly ridden, cause no more erosion than feet.

⚙ **What you need:** A high quality mountain bike and Chapter 5. ⚙

Trick cyclists

Balance and co-ordination are the keys to riding a bike fast over rough terrain. Develop those qualities to a higher level and you can make a mountain bike do almost anything. Those who enjoy it call it awesome, those who don't call it showing off.

Whatever your attitude, trick riding is spectacular and those who can do it are also very fast riders on technical terrain. Champion downhill riders often start off this way.

Appeals to the daring, the natural gymnast and, er... the show-off. It appeals to young riders because it's a form of bike handling that takes plenty of free time but can be mastered in a car park.

Trick riders also go for snowboarding and BMX.

⚙ **What you need:** A mountain bike. Cheaper bikes will handle tricks so long as you don't land them too hard. See Chapter 8. ⚙

Air bandits

If you ride a mountain bike fast at a natural ramp it will take off. Develop the technique, use the terrain properly and you can make a bike fly. For some riders spectacular jumps are the biggest buzz of all.

The world height record for a jump without a ramp is almost 40in. The long jump record (off a ramp into water) is 37ft.

This sort of riding can be done in a small area and is a good way of having fun and building technique when you've only got an hour or so. Any bit of rough ground will do, or the local BMX track.

Top downhillers learn to jump so they can control the air-time they take on big courses at 50mph plus (and they love it).

⚙ **What you need:** A high quality mountain bike with heavy duty equipment. See Chapter 8. ⚙

X-country racer

Racing a mountain bike across country takes all the handling skills of the mountain biker combined with the fitness of the road racer. To get to the top requires a high degree of rigorous training and real dedication.

However, three hours at near maximum effort is only necessary for the highly motivated. There are all sorts of races for riders at different levels.

Most people race for fun. And there is a lot of fun to be had, on and off the course. Hanging out with other riders around the races is the major attraction, gossiping, raving, flirting and showing off one way or another is high on the agenda at any race series.

⚙ **What you need:** A quality mountain bike, reasonable fitness and Chapter 6. ⚙

You don't have to be screaming fit to go mountain bike racing. There are races for riders of all levels – just grab your bike and go.

Downhilling

Riding a bike as fast as you can down a mountain (or even a hillside) takes a special sort of attitude. Downhillers are in it for the adrenalin, the challenge and the free ride. They're the sort of people who surf, free-

Mountain biking nirvana. After a hard day in the saddle comes the chance to kick back and relax.

climb, ski and jump out of trees so they can crash down through the branches.

It's all about speed.

Most downhills are run against the clock, but what downhillers really like are head to head races, weaving round poles in a dual slalom or going against each other in a race like the infamous Dual Eliminator held on America's Mammoth Mountain.

TV loves the gladiatorial swagger and danger of downhill racing. The big races are on scary mountains, but British race series produce manageable courses.

☼ **What you need:** A high quality mountain bike with very heavy duty equipment. See Chapter 7. ☼

Commuting

The mountain bike has a more upright riding position than the road bike and is strong enough to survive all those big holes in the tarmac and kerb hits. That's why most commuters use some sort of a mountain bike.

Big knobbly tyres create lots of rolling resistance for no gain on tarmac, so they're best changed for slicks pumped up good and hard. Mountain bike slicks roll well but are fat enough to absorb the bumps and pits. The low gearing is high enough for most city commuting speeds most of the time. There are special racks and mudguards made for the mountain bike which turn it into a pretty good workhorse.

And the great thing about it is that you can use the bike off-road at weekends.

☼ **What you need:** A reasonable quality mountain bike, a change of clothes and Chapter 4. ☼

Downhill racing requires split second reactions, nerves of steel and a good supply of clean underwear.

Riding the world

You can ride your mountain bike away from your front door and return from the other direction, having cycled around the world. The good thing is you can start off gently and get fitter as you go.

If there's anywhere left on the planet that a mountain bike hasn't reached there's one heading for it as we speak. From tours in Europe to mammoth trips along the Andes, across the Himalayas into Tibet, across the Sahara and across the African continent... it's being done all the time.

Most of the roads in the world are dirt track, so the mountain bike is the obvious choice. Plus, if you hit a war zone or get fed up with the endless

headwind riding up from Tierra del Fuego, you can put the bike on a truck or a plane and move on.

☼ **What you need:** A good quality steel mountain bike with top quality components, the right attitude and Chapter 5. ☼

Dirty weekends

Kids love riding off-road too, so easy rides in the countryside at weekends are perfect for families so long as they are properly equipped. Children should have mountain bikes that fit them and women should have equipment, especially saddles, that are designed for them. All you need then is a bike rack for the car, a picnic basket and plenty of give and take.

Closer to home, check out the riding on the commons, the parks and canal towpaths (you'll need a permit to ride towpaths, but they're flat, near the water and pass innumerable pubs so it's worth it).

A more pleasantly relaxing way of spending a warm afternoon while getting enough exercise to work up a thirst has not yet been invented.

☼ **What you need:** Mountain bikes, plenty of tools and Chapter 3. ☼

The bike with attitude

The mountain bike does all the things discussed so far and a lot more besides – they've been jumped out of aeroplanes, ridden underwater, dragged along by parachute and jumped 100ft into the sea...

You can do all of these things and get fed up with all of them, but you'll still have the bike.

The moment you throw a leg over one you come seat to seat with an amazing piece of engineering. The MTB is the most efficient machine for turning human muscle power into forward motion over mountain and moor, through mud and rockfields, to the ends of the earth (or the chip shop), ever made. It is a portable, non-polluting, free to run piece of engineering that everyone who isn't totally decrepit ought to have.

Even if you just go down to the shops on it instead of taking the car, you score, the environment scores, we all score.

☼ What you need: A bike! ☼

Go where the wind blows. There is nothing quite as satisfying as finding a new trail.

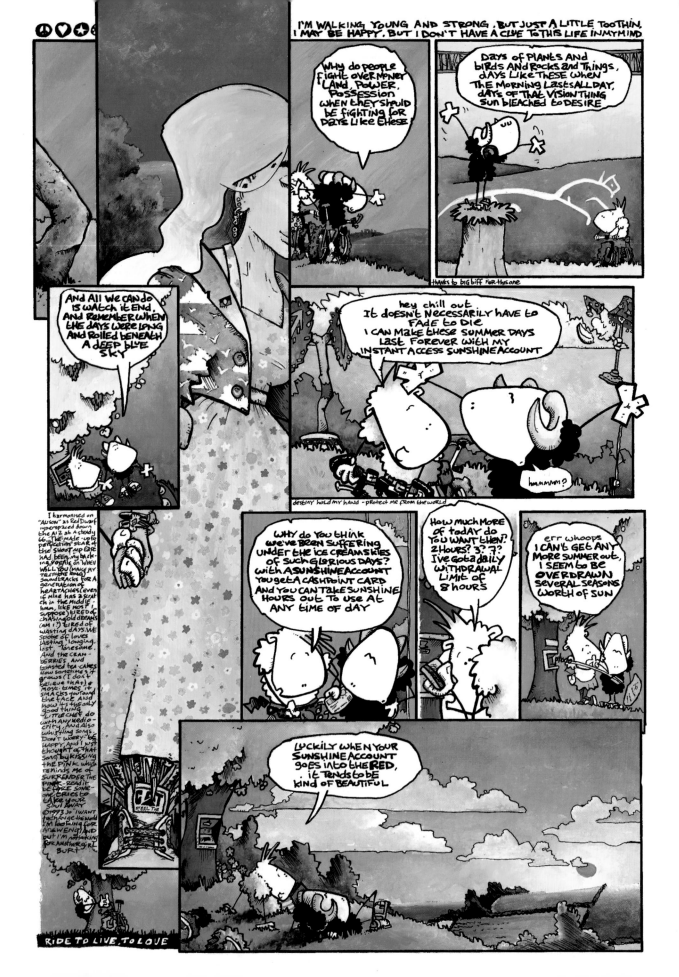

Are you a Cavalier or a Roundhead? An air bandit or a trail hound? The great thing about mountain biking is there's room for both.

A matter of attitude

How you choose to use your bike depends on your character and attitude to life. It goes deep into the British social and political divide which has been around since the Civil War.

It's an individualistic, self-sufficient culture, mountain biking. Owning an MTB symbolises a rejection of regimentation. We don't join clubs with mandates and AGMs like the roadies do. Most 'clubs' are small groups of friends. And we don't race all that seriously. It's true, races get impressive numbers of entrants, but compared to the our numbers it's a minority interest, particularly if you divide the serious racers from those who go for the peripheral fun.

We compete all right, but against the terrain and ourselves far more than against other riders. It's riding out there that brings the satisfaction, the pleasure and the fun.

Which brings me to the way people enjoy their riding. There are two extremes: the fashionable and daring who live for the adrenalin thrills of downhill, big jumps and tricks, and the performance rider who goes for hard work, high fitness, long distances and the triumph of mind over matter. It's Cavaliers and Roundheads, really, the two extremes of the British character. You can bridge the gap, but we all tend to one side or the other.

That's something that goes back to the beginning of mountain biking.

Back to The Year Clunk.

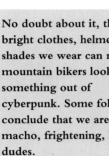

SPIRIT OF MINT

No doubt about it, the bright clothes, helmets and shades we wear can make mountain bikers look like something out of cyberpunk. Some folk conclude that we are macho, frightening, heavy dudes.

Until they see Mint Sauce! Because the hero of British mountain biking is not some hard, tough super-twonk, it's, er, a cartoon sheep.

The most popular part of Britain's most popular bike mag, Mint is an emotional, nature-loving, thin-legged philosopher who, try as he might, cannot kick his fixation with expensive bikes.

If you want to know what mountain biking is really about, then Jo Burt's gentle, introspective, hippy sheep is your best guide.

THE YEAR CLUNK

Mountain biking started as a carefree, hedonistic substitute for skiing amongst the Marin mountains in seventies California. You can get serious about the game, but it will always be gonzo at heart.

People have been riding bicycles off-road since the things were invented, but the guys who caught the wave which led to mountain biking as we know it came out of Marin County California in the seventies (the accent's on the second syllable, Mar-IN, by the way). They rode old bikes, what they called Clunkers, down mountains, back in the year Clunk.

Those people are still mountain bikers, they've still got that wild look in their eyes, and their suits can't hide the fact that they were a lot more comfortable in jeans, the right leg ragged and oiled up from the chainring.

Here's a few names to conjure with: Gary Fisher, Joe Breeze, Joe Murray, Jacquie Phelan, Charlie Cunningham, Charles Kelly, Tom Ritchey...

The mountains around Marin County are just across the Bay from San Fransisco and it's one hell of a place to ride. In the early seventies a bunch of these guys started taking ancient balloon-tyred bicycles up the mountains and dropping them down 1000ft of mountainside in around five minutes with top speeds up around 60mph.

None of this nonsense about riding uphill then. You hauled the bikes up in a truck. It was all about speed and exhilaration – besides, the bikes weighed a ton and had only one gear.

Joke bikes

The truth is the mountain bike evolved from the least efficient bicycle ever made. Around the thirties, when Henry Ford's tin boxes started knocking bikes off the road, American companies came out with these low pressure balloon-tyred jobs, based on the low pressure car tyres fashionable at the time, and made them look like motorbikes – they had false tanks, mudguards, chainguards, built in lights, bells, whistles...

They also only had one gear, one coaster (back pedal) brake on the rear, and one-size frames which used long bendy seatposts to fit big guys.

The American bike industry made these things for thirty years and the good thing about them was they were cheap (people'd give them away).

The Repack

Everyone thought Joe and Charlie and Gary were crazy, but they were so laid back they were almost horizontal and it was cool.

Believe it or not this bunch of unlikely looking characters are the guys who invented the sport we know today as mountain biking. Honest, it's true.

But of course they wanted to know who got down the trails fastest, so the Repack race was invented, a time trial down a trail which fell around 1300ft in two miles and was remote enough to get away with such a dangerous activity.

The Repack (called that because a rider claimed his single rear brake got so hot he had to re-pack it with grease after every run) became a series. And it formed the focus for improved equipment.

Gary Fisher started modifying his clunker – front brake, front derailleur (to keep the chain on), then a five speed coaster brake hub, thumbshifters on the widest possible bars – most of the stuff was adapted motorcycle gear. Gary introduced the seatpost quick release, simply because the posts bent if you sat on them down the Repack and he wanted the thing out of the way.

Hello mountain bike
Fisher still holds the record for the fastest time down the Repack. Joe Breeze was second fastest. Joe had built road frames and started work on

a bike especially to compete in the race. It took him eight months because nothing existed to fit the fat tyres, but once one was built the next ten followed quickly.

Joe introduced cantilever brakes, flat handlebars and the diamond frame. That was 1976.

The bikes were test-ridden by the Marin fanatics and Joe saw what needed to be improved. He discussed the bike with Tom Ritchey, already a respected frame builder who lived 50 miles south of Marin. Tom caught on straightaway and built three frames. He sold one to Gary Fisher, kept one and Gary sold the third.

Inspired by the project, Ritchey built another nine frames in different sizes and colours. About the only place you could sell them was Marin County, so Gary Fisher and Charles Kelly started a company called MountainBikes, to sell them.

Ritchey built the frames, Kelly and Fisher assembled the bikes from an odd mix of BMX, motorcycle and race bike parts, suitably adapted.

That was 1979, the year alloy rims became available and took 3lbs off

each wheel.

In 1980 Specialized produced a mountain bike based pretty closely on the Ritchey design. In 1981 they made the first production mountain bike, The Stumpjumper.

In '82 Shimano and SunTour produced the first MTB groupsets, everything took off, prices came down, and mountain biking was GO.

The work ethic

In Britain too, people had been riding bikes off-road for years and bikes were being designed specially for the purpose. But the American production bikes really started things happening.

In those days races were more like parties, a chance to meet your friends, party and race (more often than not with a hangover).

But more bikes meant more competition and competition demands rules and a governing body. The American founding fathers started NORBA (a commercial company in the best US tradition), but if there was to be international competition mountain biking had to deal with the world governing body, the UCI.

The UCI, based in Switzerland, comes out of the European road racing tradition and road racing is not about partying and having fun. It's about training, dedication, half killing yourself and winning.

Come the first World Championship NORBA had to stamp its feet very hard to preserve downhill racing as a rainbow jersey event at all. Suddenly cross-country racing was mountain biking.

Tim Gould and David Baker from cyclo-cross were the first pukka cyclists to hit British racing. Riding bikes like bedsteads they put five minutes into the top mountain bikers.

The work ethic arrived. Stretched out riding positions, aping road racing, became fashionable. Riders trained on the road. Everyone got very serious about what they now called 'the sport'.

A UCI-recognised body took control of mountain biking in Britain. At their first meeting they discussed how *MBUK*, a magazine that always kept a place in its heart for the gonzo side of mountain biking, could be prevented from presenting a 'bad image' of 'the sport'.

Bad news. It looked like the road cycling roundheads, more renowned for their blazers than their sense of humour, were in the box seat.

Saved by the box

It didn't happen, though. Leaders almost always have to follow, and for the bulk of people who were into mountain bikes all over the world, it wasn't a sport, it was an activity and it was fun. They were in it to enjoy the countryside, get fit, scream downhill, jump, play around and enjoy themselves.

Er, sometimes the urge to do something stupid with your bike is so strong it just overcomes you. Don't try to fight it.

THE REAL MOUNTAIN BIKER

Anyone can buy a mountain bike and pedal it. Being a real mountain biker is a bit more difficult than that. Of course, you don't have to be cool, but it helps.

<u>Look after the earth</u> – when you know how to ride you can pass over the ground so lightly no one knows you've been.

<u>Look after people</u> – when you ride the road you know what it's like to be terrorised by careless, short-sighted, arrogant drivers. On the trails, you're the overtaking traffic. Don't make like a Volvo twonk.

<u>Look after yourself</u> – there are sad people about who like to take out their inadequacies on anyone who's different. Some like to shout at mountain bikers. Just smile and move on – let them get the ulcers. That's it really.

They knew what the TV people saw the moment they looked at mountain biking, that the drama of cross-country racing was experienced more by the riders than by onlookers.

For TV, downhill was the thing and head-to-head downhill for choice. Big jumps, amazing tricks and staggering scenery are the visual signs of the freedom and excitement of mountain biking.

Getting it together

So if you're only just getting into mountain biking, you're coming in at a time when the original gonzo spirit of it all is right back at the heart of the matter, where it belongs. Almost everything you can do on a mountain bike is OK to do and you'll find people to do it with.

Even our access to the countryside, which has produced more sensational nonsense in the press than real problems on the ground, is being discussed more sensibly as other countryside users realise what mountain biking really is.

It doesn't really matter which side of the Roundhead/Cavalier thing you tend to, we're all mountain bikers. This book is going to tell you everything that you need to know to get into the mountain bike thang, starting right now in Chapter 2.

C H A P T E R   2

kitting out

THE BIKE YOU NEED, THE TECHNICAL

FACTS, BUYING IT,

SETTING IT UP, ALL THE RIGHT KIT

Engineer, inventor, Disc Jockey and curry fanatic and owner of Ben a black and tan collie. Brant Richards is the Technical Editor of *MBUK* and regular contributor to *MTB Pro* magazine. Yorkshire all over – he carries most of it splattered up his back. Fine technical rider too.

The basics

There's a lot of rubbish talked about mountain bikes. Get talking to bikaholics and they'll tell you certain bikes 'have soul', others 'have no soul', and yet others 'seem to ride themselves'.

Garbage, I reckon. And about as much use to someone getting into mountain biking as a chocolate teapot.

It may mean something to arty types, but I'm an engineer and I come from Yorkshire, so we'll have none of that here.

What most mountain bikes really are is a collection of tubes stuck together one way or another, with bits bolted on so they stop and go and turn corners properly.

They're engineered out of metal, plastic and rubber. If you can't cold forge it, join it together effectively or CNC machine it, it's not there, and no one's learned to engineer 'soul'.

Rather special tubes

The most important part of a bike is the frame. Most frames are made from a collection of tubes (a tubeset) which is specifically designed for bike frames. The most common materials are some form of steel, some form of aluminium and some form of titanium (composites and plastics are being used more, but are much less common).

One good thing about the mountain bike industry is that you get what you pay for. Basically, the more expensive the bike is, the better quality the frame material is.

What do I mean by 'quality'? Good question. When it comes to bikes the quality of a frame material is governed by its mechanical integrity. The properties of the material itself, strength and stiffness, are important, but don't mean a thing unless the material can be welded together effectively.

What we are looking for in a bike frame is a strong structure which is as light as it can possibly be – or in the real world, as light as the customer

Titanium frames are expensive, strong, light, won't rust and, better than all that, they make your mates dribble.

is prepared to pay for it to be. You pay more for less material and less weight, and when you've ridden light and heavy bikes you know that it's worth it.

Let's look at the common materials:

STEEL: It's cheap and easy to work with so less expensive bikes are made from steel. But there are different qualities of steel.

Really cheap steel, more suited to garden furniture, and really quite weak, is used to make really cheap mountain bikes. Because the steel is weak the framebuilder has to use a lot of it to get a frame that's strong enough to last any length of time, so it weighs a ton.

All steels have the same density – a brick of the cheapest, nastiest steel weighs the same as a brick of best quality high strength jet-fighter steel. Better quality steel frames weigh (a lot) less because top quality material can be used to make tubes with thinner walls.

The thickness of the walls in top quality steel tubesets vary – the ends,

DOUBLE BUTTED

JARGON BUSTER

A quality bike frame tube is far thinner than you may think. A typical steel tube is a maximum of 1mm thick, and usually a lot thinner, certainly in the centre. Butting is the process of changing a tube's wall thickness internally, without altering its outside diameter. A tube is said to be 'double butted' if it has this change at both ends. Yes, it's a good thing.

where they're welded, have more metal in the walls, which are thinned towards the centre of the tube, saving weight and adding resilience to the frame. This internal shaping is known as 'butting', and is used on the better quality framesets.

ALUMINIUM: The cheapest of the alternative materials, aluminium offers increased stiffness, which means less muscle power is lost bending the frame but the ride is harsher. Although lighter than steel it is weaker so more has to be used. Large diameter aluminium tubes give a strong frame with a weight advantage over steel.

TITANIUM: Much the same feel as steel, slightly more resilient and very light. For some people it's the dream metal, and it costs more than you'd dream of too.

CARBON: Now being used both in tube and moulded form. It rides well, but it's too early to tell how it will perform long-term.

Aluminium Extreme Klein frames are aluminium works of art.

The Specialized FSR – lightweight steel AND full suspension, phew.

Shimano XTR is the pinnacle of mountain bike componentry.

THE ESSENTIAL PARTS

Gears

A lot of homage is paid to the gear system of the mountain bike, but it's really a clumsy, archaic system of levers, bits of wire and pivoting linkages. The lever on the handlebar pulls a pre-set length of cable through the outer cables on the frame, moving the gear mechanism which pushes the chain brutally from one sprocket to another. Push it on to a sprocket with fewer teeth and the wheel will go round faster but will be harder to push and vice versa. Victorian technology.

Although the main manufacturer, Shimano, has made improvements in tooth profiles to make all that happen very efficiently, it's still an inelegant solution to the problem in engineering terms. But it's simple, pretty cheap to make and it works.

Because it has to handle such a variety of conditions, from steep uphills on very unhelpful surfaces, to fast, well surfaced track, the mountain bike needs a wide range of gears, which inevitably leads to wide gaps between ratios.

Three chainrings at the front and a cassette of six, seven or eight sprockets at the back is what's on offer. The more sprockets the smoother the change between ratios, but seven is adequate for most purposes.

There are two standards of gearing coexisting. The 'compact drive' standard typically gives you 22/32/42 chainrings at the front and an 11-28 back cassette, giving lower lows and higher highs. Older bikes, or models still using the original standard, generally have 26/36/46 chainrings and a 12-28 cassette.

When you've ridden long enough to get fit you should be able to deal with flat, off-road terrain in the middle chainring and climb most things in the small (granny) ring. If you can't, you probably need smaller rings. Your local dealer will get you sorted.

Consider your gearing as three sets of seven (or eight gears). Use the rear changer until you're forced to go to a smaller or bigger chainring. The

front changer makes a big jump in your gearing which you would generally only use, outside this sort of sequence, when the terrain goes violently up or down.

Brakes

Mountain bike brakes are very simple. A lever mounted on the handlebar pulls a cable through an outer, hauling the blocks against the rim. Proper mountain bikes use 'cantilever' brakes, which mount to bosses, welded on

ANATOMY OF THE BIKE

A Rear sprockets

B Rear dropout

C Rear mech

D Front mech

E Chainset and, behind, bottom bracket

F Stem

G Brake and gear levers

H Headset

I Front cantilever brake

J Front dropout

K Rear cantilever brake

L Bar ends

M Front suspension fork

to the frame tubes. They're more rigid than one-piece units, bolted through the fork or stays, that road bikes use. They also give better mud clearance, and allow braking even with buckled wheels.

Wheels

Again, old technology, but the spoked wheel is a marvel of engineering. Wheels take an inordinate amount of hammer, provided the tension in the spokes is correct. Check for equal spoke tension regularly by plucking them. They won't make the same sound, but you'll find the loose ones.

Light wheels are a double benefit. Not only do they reduce the all-up weight of the bike, but you expend less effort turning them. Like everything else with bikes, light kit costs. Get the lightest wheels that you can afford.

ADVANCED TECHNOLOGY

Front suspension

Suspension forks are now well enough developed to be a desirable upgrade for most riders. Essentially they delay and smooth out the transmission of front wheel impacts to bike and rider, making your bike more comfortable, more controllable and letting you ride faster.

To do this they use some sort of spring and some form of damping to stop the spring rebounding with the same speed and force with which it was compressed, like a pogostick.

The materials used fall into three categories: elastomer (spring and damping), elastomer spring/oil damping and air spring/oil damping.

Elastomer forks use small rubber-like bumpers to act as a spring. The special compound used has an inherent natural damping property that stops it bouncing back hard as, say, a steel spring would.

Elastomer/oil forks use similar bumpers as the spring, but control the damping characteristics

For general trail riding, any old mountain bike will do. Be more specific when your riding gets more specific.

Judy isn't the name of my sister but the name of the new Rock Shox suspension fork.

more precisely with a hydraulic cartridge.

Air/oil forks use air as the spring and oil damping to control the movement.

Pros and cons: Hydraulic damping offers better control of fork movement than a pure elastomer unit, but it requires more maintenance.

Changing the oil in a hydraulic fork isn't a tough job, it's no harder than filling a kettle, but it's unlike anything else you need to do to a mountain bike, which scares some people.

Rear suspension

Front suspension is pretty much sorted and rear suspension is settling down. There are far fewer ridiculous concepts around. Most of the full suspension bikes now on the market have been developed over a number of years and work well.

Some are designed as cross-country machines, some are downhill specials. It's more usual to see full suspension bikes in downhill races than it is to see them being ridden cross-country, but the benefits of better traction and superior comfort make a good full suspension cross-country bike an attractive proposition.

The downside is extra weight, complexity and difficult maintenance. The perfectly sorted full-floating suspension bike is the machine of the future, but for the average rider it's a few years away yet.

✿ For more detail on advanced gear see Chapter 9. ✿

BUYING A BIKE

What do you really need?

There are only two types of mountain bike – good ones and bad ones.

There's no such thing as a touring, racing, jumping or going-down-the-shops mountain bike. What you want from your bike is what everyone wants: it must be light, strong, efficient and reliable, and you want that no matter what you're going to use it for.

Good bikes cost more than bad bikes. It really is

that simple in a well sorted market which is carefully monitored by dedicated testers working for the magazines (er, like me, blush).

You can have lots of fun and learn plenty on a cheap bike, one of the things you learn being the advantages of a better machine.

Low weight, strength and efficiency are factors of price, but reliability is generally pretty good. Shimano is the dominant market force in componentry across almost all the bikes on the market and their stuff is good. The more expensive component ranges, like Deore XT and XTR, are very reliable, but many of the features that we cried out for in years gone by are now available on entry-level bikes.

The right bike for you

What's the right size: A mountain bike needs to fit you. Too big and you'll crunch yourself on the top tube when you have to jump off the saddle. Too small and you'll be cramped up and unable to get the best out of your riding.

If you straddle a bike which is the right size, with your feet flat on the ground, you will have at least 3in of clearance between your crotch and the top-tube.

It's not just the height of the frame that's important. The distance from the saddle to the handlebar affects how comfortable the bike is too. Your body and arms should make a right angle when you are sitting on the saddle firmly gripping the bars.

Women generally have shorter torsos for their height, and so often need a shorter top-tube length than a similarly sized man.

Children must have bikes that fit them – now. If you're buying a bike for a kid, or are a kid buying a bike, don't get one that's too big. Kids can grow into anoraks or shoes, not bikes. They can do themselves serious damage waiting to grow into a big bike.

The re-sale market for second-hand kids bikes is good, so keep them in good nick and replace them as they are outgrown.

Where to buy it: Bike shops are the only places to buy mountain bikes. Unlike tomato plants and barbecues, bikes need to be properly assembled,

Unless you get the right size bike you won't be able to go flat out in comfort.

tested, checked and serviced. Don't buy your bike from a garage, or a DIY shop, or a mail-order-clothing catalogue. The best bike shops are those that come with a recommendation. Enthusiasts soon find out the good shops. Ask around at work, ask friends, stop mountain bikers in the street. The shop you buy from is as important as the bike you buy.

Should I buy second hand: The second hand mountain bike market is large and thriving. Folks are always wanting to upgrade their bike, or parts of their bike for new kit, and there are real deals to be had.

Generally look at paying around half the retail price for a second-hand bike that's had a year of use.

You need to take care, of course. Some riders use their bikes a lot, some don't. Some folks who use their bikes a lot look after them better than others.

It's easy to make a shoddy bike look good on the surface, but a knowledgeable friend should be able to spot the gems from the horse muck. A mate who knows a crown-race from a cotter-pin is worth his or her weight in gold when buying second-hand.

What should I spend: As much as you can afford. In mountain bikes more money buys better quality. At the time of writing, and for the foreseeable future, £350 buys the sort of bike that won't fall apart rapidly off-road. From there on in, more money buys a better bike, although you start to get diminishing returns on your money after around £800. After that the improvements get smaller and the average rider may not find the extra money buys tangible benefits.

Setting it all up

Bike set-up means adjusting the contact points on the machine – saddle, bar and controls – so you can use it at maximum efficiency. Incorrect set-

If you're happy and you know it, do a trick. Mountain biking is about having fun. If you haven't joined us yet, you're missing out.

up wastes energy, can make the bike tricky to handle and, at worst, can be life threatening.

Saddle position

You can adjust your saddle three ways: the post can be raised or lowered to give the correct leg extension during the pedalling stroke, the saddle can be moved backwards or forwards in the seatpost clamp, to fine tune the distance from the saddle to the bar and it can be angled for comfort.

It's best to ignore all the precise methods that come from road racing. Absolute positioning makes sense on a road bike, which is a machine designed to extract the maximum from the rider, but you're never in one position for long on a mountain bike. So forget absolute anatomical efficiency, just get comfortable.

The right height:

The most important thing is to get the right saddle height. If this isn't correct your knees won't extend correctly through the pedalling stroke, which can damage them. Here's how to get it right:

Sit squarely in the saddle, leaning against a wall for support, and get the crank arms in line with the seat tube. Place your heel on the lower pedal and move the saddle up or down until your leg is completely straight. Now when you move your foot into the correct pedalling position, with the ball of the foot in the centre of the pedal, your leg should be almost straight but not quite.

When the position is right you can only get a tip-toe on the ground when in the saddle. This is fine. This is how it should be.

Caution: If you find that to get the correct saddle height the post is either almost out of the frame completely (check for the MAX HEIGHT line on the post), or all the way into the frame, then something's wrong. All the way out means you either have a very small frame, or a very short seatpost. If you need a post longer than 350mm, your frame is too small for you. If you only have 2in of post showing, you have a frame that's too big for you.

Exceptions: When riding very rough terrain, when you are often out of the saddle or descending steep slopes, it pays to drop your saddle a touch. Around 1-2in is normal, depending on the nature of the terrain.

Saddle to bar adjustment:

Moving your weight about out of the saddle is the key to controlling a bike off-road. Most riders simply push their saddles all the way back on the rails to lengthen the bar-saddle distance and give them room to move.

Angle adjustment:

Saddle angle can be altered by adjusting the cradle that the seat sits in on

Getting the saddle and the bar in the right postion will make climbing and descending an easier and more comfortable experience.

UPGRADE PRIORITIES

Most new riders will buy a bike with a steel or aluminium frame. Manufacturers have two ways of hitting the price they think you can afford. They can mix a superior frame with inferior components or the other way around. Study the magazines and go for the best frame you can afford. Upgrade the components as they wear out.

Everything on your bike can be interchanged and upgraded and lighter/better components are coming on to the market all the time. Some of it improves your bike's performance, a lot of it doesn't. The magazines are your number one source for new component information.

If you want to upgrade, get the contact points of the bike sorted out. Customise where the bike touches you and the ground, and you'll get much better performance.

HERE'S A HIT LIST:
- Good quality tyres
- Bar ends
- Stem to suit
- Good saddle
- Clipless pedals
- Suspension fork
- Strong, light wheels

top of the seatpost. Exact details vary from post to post, but the basic trick is to loosen the bolt under the saddle and wag the post around until you get the saddle where you want it. Then tighten the bolt back up, tightly.

Small adjustments for comfort are OK, but keep it as flat as you can. Lots of tilt either way puts strain on the body and pressure on important nerve channels.

Handlebar position

You can alter the position of your bars in three ways:

Bar profile: Rotating the bar in the stem clamp alters its profile. Take it from one who's tried them all — clamp your bar with the backswept curve in line with your arms as it was designed to be and leave it there!

Bar height: There are two common ways of attaching a stem to the fork steerer tube — the old expander bolt style and the new Aheadset system. With an expander bolt (all you see is an allen key slotted bolt head which goes through the stem into the steerer), you can raise or lower the stem a

With your skills up to scratch you can really let rip, like Jason McRoy.

little in the steerer tube. With the Aheadset, which uses a stem that clamps on to the fork steerer tube, you can't. You need a different stem. Don't alter your stem without advice unless you really know what you're doing – a good shop will be able to help, not only with product choice, but also with set-up tips.

When adjusting your stem, try positioning your bar 2-3in lower than your saddle. Any higher than this and you'll start to loop out backwards on climbs; any lower and you can't see where you're going.

Control position

Almost all new bikes come with brake levers and shift levers as one unit, which limits adjustment. Brake levers should point downwards at roughly 30-45 degrees. Get them in line with your arms in the riding position so you don't have to swivel your wrists on the bars to grab them.

SET UP FOR A PURPOSE

A good bike is a good bike and you adapt it to suit your kind of riding. Here are three set up for specific purposes:

Cross-country race bike

The long, low stem puts the racer in an aerodynamic position similar to

that on the road bike which he or she will train on, allowing him to get his head down and hammer on the flats and climbs. The position does compromise handling in downhill situations, but cross-country races aren't often won on downhills.

Downhill bike

A big, curvy, upswept handlebar and a low saddle sets the bike up for manoeuvrability at high speed. The bar is wide and high to give excellent control, and the saddle's dropped to give the rider room to move about when coming off those big drops. Flat pedals are also used sometimes to make foot-down cornering easier.

General trail bike

A wide handlebar coupled to a high stem gives control and comfort for uphill or downhill riding. Using a mixture of influences from downhill and cross-country racing, true trail riders fettle their bikes to give excellent control in all the situations that they're likely to meet. So, if you spend most of your time on flat trails you'll veer towards the cross-country set-up, and so on.

Once your bike is set up correctly so you can learn techniques correctly, the sky is very much the limit.

ESSENTIAL KIT

As well as the mass of stuff to make your bike perform better, there's a welter of kit aimed at making you more efficient and comfortable – helmets and other protective garb, extreme weather clothing, shades, bags, tools, computers, drinking systems, guide books, waterproof boots, full face helmets...

A lot of it is specialist kit. Here's the minimum that you should look at getting when you start mountain biking for real:

Helmet: If you never ever buy anything else for your bike make sure you have one of these. You WILL crash and all serious riders will admit helmets have saved them from serious injury.

The helmets you will find on sale here are rated by two American standards – Snell and ANSI – and our own British Standard. All have slightly different criteria for helmet safety, but most people are agreed that Snell is the most stringent.

Check inside the helmet for a blue Snell sticker and then check to see if the helmet fits. Different brands of helmet fit different shaped heads. If your bonce just doesn't fit inside a Vetta, say, try a Bell.

Starting off at around twenty five quid, a helmet is the first purchase any prospective mountain biker should make.

And remember, they don't last for ever. I trash a helmet at least once a year, either by complete destruction or because I'm concerned about its strength after a few small bumps.

Some fools moan about paying twenty five pounds for 'a lump of polystyrene', but a helmet is so much more than that. Just as you've got to have insurance for a car, consider this insurance for your head.

Gloves: If you don't land on your head

An expensive helmet is still cheaper than hospital treatment.

Shades protect your eyes from flying nasties as well as sun.

Full finger gloves will save your hands when you fall.

when you crash, you'll land on your hands. Without some form of glove you'll rip your palms to shreds and leave interesting flappy bits of skin blowing in the breeze. Ouch!

Gloves come fingerless and fingered, in summer and winter weights. Get an appropriate pair straightaway. As well as protecting your palms from the trail, they make holding on to handlebars easier.

Eyewear: Bugs, sun, rain, slime and small family pets leap up and try to make a home in your eyes when you're riding. You need eye protection and normal shades don't have everything that the mountain biker needs. Here's what you should be looking for: lenses made of plastic and not glass, so they don't cut your eyes if you stack up badly; frames made of plastic too for the same reason; a lens profile and lens to face fit that stops flying grit getting in your peepers; and lens material that is a true UV filter, to limit the chances of contracting retinal cancer.

Top glasses manufacturers include Arnet, Bloc, Bollé, JT and Oakley.

Boots: Always wear specialist MTB boots when out on the trail. You may think your attractive, designer label, high-top tanbucks or funky air-cushioned pumps are the business for mountain biking, but I'm here to tell you they're not. Proper mountain bike boots not only protect your ankles and toes from the abuse of off-road debris, but they also have a sole that doesn't soak up pedalling effort and lets you hammer the pedals without the pedals hammering you. Prices for good boots start at around £40.

Shorts: A helmet is essential but a pair of good cycling shorts comes a very close second. The secret is a

Steve 'Rugged and Windswept' Worland never rides without his safety gear.

A stout pair of bike shoes is essential out in the wilds.

synthetic chamois padded insert combined with proper cut and seaming (different for men and women) so they don't chafe you when you ride, but allow free movement.

Lycra blends are the materials of choice, but touring shorts are available which have a baggy appearance, with a suspended inner short for those who don't want to look too obviously like cyclists. Short liners are also on the market which are a cut-down lightweight bike short, allowing you to ride in conventional athletic wear.

Shorts will seriously improve the comfort on your bike, but don't expect miracles. The human body does require a little 'toughening up' before getting used to life in the saddle, so a little soreness is common. Anything that numbs parts of the body or causes severe chafing should be investigated.

Cycling shorts are designed to be worn next to the skin, with no underwear, so it's sensible (and hygienic) to buy two pairs if you're going to ride frequently.

CHAPTER 3

go do it

FINDING RIDES, LEGAL AND

ECO CONSIDERATIONS,

GETTING FIT, BASIC

RIDING TECHNIQUE

Enthusiasm incarnate, Derek Purdy is MBUK's wilderness specialist. Drawn to the mountains, he likes to ride as high as possible. Happiest sheltering behind a dry stone wall in a blizzard, sharing his sandwiches with a weasel.

If you've read this book from the start you'll have seen all the inspirational stuff from Tym about the huge variety of pleasure mountain biking can give you and the news from Brant that all you need to enjoy them is a good bike.

Then you get to me and the hard work begins!

No, it doesn't have to be that hard, but there's no getting away from the fact that, no matter what type of riding attracts you, you can't develop the skills or the fitness to get the internal grin we all talk about going, without doing a fair bit of riding.

And the first question every new rider wants answered is: where am I going to ride my bike? Don't worry, finding places to ride which comply with legal, safety and ecological considerations isn't too difficult once you get into the groove of looking and realise what your bike will do.

Cityscapes

It's more difficult, of course, if you have no car, little money and live in a city. But you're not the only rider around, so the obvious thing is to find out where everyone else rides. Bike shops come in here, they're not only the best place to buy bikes, they're centres for information like this. Mountain bikers hang around mountain bike shops, get in on the gossip!

There are plenty of urban options:

Concrete and tarmac: Roads are dirty, smelly, full of cars and a tad boring, but the top racers get in most of their fitness training on tarmac. And top trick riders learnt their skills in car parks and paved areas.

Anyway, tarmac is the best place to learn how your gears work and how your bike handles, and to start getting in a bit of bike fitness.

Waste ground: Around most urban areas there is waste ground of one sort or another, ranging from bumpy bits yet to be built on to vast pit heaps which will provide lots of entertainment, teach you amazing handling skills and tire you out quicker than circuit training!

Avoid quarries, unless they are very old and weathered and well tried out by other riders. There could well be loose rock lurking to trap the unwary,

You don't have to go off-road to have fun. Once you've developed a few skills, you'll see your urban environment in a totally new light.

Open, urban spaces are just the places to perfect and perform eye-catching tricks and manoeuvres.

and we don't like losing readers over the edge.

Of course a lot of wasteland is hazardous. The downside of urban waste ground is that it becomes a dump full of broken metalwork and glass, which wrecks bikes and bodies.

The key to finding places like this which are safe and open for riding is local knowledge and local riders.

BMX tracks: Not so many as there were, but a good track is excellent for learning handling skills.

Cycle tracks: Thanks to Sustrans (it stands for Sustainable Transport and does something about it) and various local authorities, many defunct railway lines have been converted into great cycle tracks. They are traffic free, usually have a good firm base, but they're off-road riding and, when

wet, will get you satisfactorily dirty. Great escape routes from city or town. Ring your local council for information on your area.

Canal towpaths: Another escape route, cutting through many of our industrial towns and cities, is the canal. You need a permit to cycle the towpaths, but they are a green lifeline going through the heart of the urban sprawl.

Countryside

If you live in or are within riding distance of the country you'll have no problems. Just get your Ordnance Survey map out and start exploring. Chapter 5 deals with the business of real off-road riding in detail. There is a huge network of trails out there, but it's important to know from the

There is nothing quite like riding off into the pale green yonder.

beginning which you are entitled to ride and which you are not.

Forest Enterprise: If you're going to take your bike out of town for the day, by car or train (bikes are carried cheaply on some trains, not on all, check with your local station) it's reassuring to know there are good trails at the end of the trip. Forest Enterprise have designated various roads within most forests as cycle routes, signposted them, and have even created link tracks to make extended rides in some cases. We can't ask better than that.

A great number of mountain bike competitions held within forest complexes use these routes, many of which are very technical and testing, well worth a visit. Further details on cycle paths in Chapter 4.

Legal considerations

In England and Wales a definitive system of Rights of Way exists, dividing tracks, paths and roads into various categories, and defining how they can be used. In most other countries the attitude is "if you can ride it, use it", but we must abide by our own law.

The situation in Scotland is slightly different. It appears a lot simpler because of the widespread belief that bicycles can be ridden wherever a path exists and, in general, this is accepted. There are local anomalies though (as usual), and you may find other interests (usually shooting or conservationist – the latter often disguised shooters) vigorously contesting the issue.

You can never tell for certain what is or is not a right of way by looking at what physically lies on the ground (or even what is written on the signs, necessarily, as footpaths are sometimes laid over other rights of way). The only certain record is the Definitive Map, but that is held by the local

PUBLIC RIGHTS OF WAY
(Not applicable to Scotland)

– – – – – – – –   Footpath

— — — — —   Bridleway

—— - —— - —— - –   Road used as a public path

+ – + – + – + -   Byway open to all traffic

Go through puddles not round them. Going round just makes them wider

county council, so you can't carry it around with you.

The safest practical method is to check with the relevant Ordnance Survey map which has a section in the key defining Public Rights Of Way. It's not foolproof, as the maps themselves make clear, but it's usually good enough.

Successful route planning depends on a good understanding of maps. This will be dealt with in Chapter 5, but there is no reason why you shouldn't get a map of your local area and start now.

LOOKING AFTER THE LAND

"All men kill the thing they love," wrote Oscar Wilde, and real mountain bikers – who go out to enjoy the unspoilt beauty of the countryside – are always concerned to leave it as unscarred as they found it.

Recent hyped-up scares in the press have caused us some concern, but now painstaking scientific research has been done by Crispin Smith, BSc (published in *MTB Pro* No 13 September 1994) and confirmed by very similar research conducted by Tanya Holdsworth BSc in the Pentland Hills.

The two studies observed the result of many passes by tyres and feet over controlled squares of terrain measuring the dispersal of surface protection and soil compaction caused by each.

The results are encouraging. Properly ridden, the mountain bike proved to cause less damage than feet in almost all circumstances.

The one exception is bikes ridden down un-vegetated hillsides. Feet tend to make holes, but tyres can form rills which lead to water erosion.

Essentially, if we stick to hard-based tracks downhill (which we normally would anyway) we cause less damage than walkers.

Which doesn't mean no damage!

Anyone who goes into the hills causes some damage. But if we ride properly, with due consideration for the conditions and types of terrain, we can minimise it.

Skids stuff

When you're out and you see bike skidmarks down every hill it's a sure thing you're following a beginner or an incompetent.

Bad braking is a common fault among the inexperienced, or plain stupid, and understandable to some degree. They come to a descent that looks too steep for them, lock on the back brake and keep it locked on, hoping that the rear wheel will hop down after them. Very often it does, very often it doesn't because they hit a damp or grassy patch, the locked wheel skids across and dumps them on to the seat of their shorts.

Group rides in the back country are great fun, but look after the land.

PUBLIC RIGHTS OF WAY

What they mean:

Footpath: A footpath is a right of way on foot, nothing else. You are not entitled to ride a bike on a footpath without the express permission of the landowner.

Bridleway: A bridleway is a right of way on foot, on horse or on a bicycle. The right to ride bikes on bridleways was extended to us in 1968 by the Countryside Act on condition we "give way to pedestrians and persons on horseback".

RUPP: Stands for Road Used as a Public Path. These are disappearing and being reclassified either as bridleways, footpaths or BOATS (see below). The right of way is confusing but, as they have been classified as a road of some sort, you are almost always OK.

BOAT: A Byway Open to All Traffic. Anything including motor vehicles can use these, so look out for the 4WDs. Usually an unsealed road and excellent riding.

Towpaths offer a traffic-free option to the town dwelling mountain biker, but remember that you do share it with walkers.

Doing it right

Use both brakes. On steep hills I usually keep my front brake moaning, just short of skidding, and do the cadence bit with the back one, choosing the firmest bits of terrain, or rock, to do the heaviest phase of the on/off sequence.

Cadence braking is rhythmic braking. Brakes are at their most effective when they are on the point of locking up, so it follows that the more frequently you can induce this condition the quicker you should stop. This is the principle behind ABS on motor vehicles.

The idea is to apply and re-apply the brakes at least once a second.

Cadence braking takes some practice. If you can't do it, scrub off speed with both brakes but keep the wheels rolling. Don't lock 'em up on the soft stuff. And if you have to scrub off a lot of speed, choose a hard bit for hard braking.

Learn your trade on hard track, keep off soft surfaces when it's wet, and see just how little trace you can leave behind you.

Wet weather terrain

When conditions are wet, particularly in winter, the sensible thing to do is ride surfaces which can take a bit of stick; firm stuff that will be least affected by the passage of a bike.

■ The most durable surface is tarmac – not only will it be ecologically friendly, it will be a lot easier too. Lots of mud really saps your strength to the point where it is not fun any more, but there are some really hairy tarmac roads, with horrendous climbs and fantastic downhills. Look for the gradient arrows on the map.

■ Old byways usually have a firm, stony base somewhere. Many have become so overgrown you will think they are a grass road. They're not going to be easy, but slot a couple of short ones into a tarmac route to raise the entertainment value and see what happens.

■ Stony tracks, regularly used by agricultural vehicles, are also a good wet weather stand-by. They require extra strength, good feel and excellent balance. A whole new technique and well worth the effort.

■ Lastly, there are the good old forest roads. Bikes do no harm to routes designed for 30 ton trucks, even in the wettest conditions.

FITNESS FACTOR

How fit do you need to be?

So long as you're in good health, you don't have to be very fit at all to start with. Unless you have a known or suspected medical condition it doesn't really matter. Older people who haven't taken much exercise for a while could reassure themselves by having a check-up before launching

Walkers aren't so much of a problem here. Gradients are, though. Get fit first.

into heavy training, but the great thing about cycling is that you get fitter as you ride.

How fit do you have to be to enjoy mountain biking to the full? The fitter the better! It's a tough sport. Apart from the obvious leg and lung fitness you need a reasonable degree of upper body strength and arm power to function properly and without undue fatigue.

No pain, no gain – you'll find early off-road rides leave you aching in the most unusual places like the neck, shoulders and the tops of your arms. This is not unusual, most folk get it when they start.

Building fitness on the bike

At the beginning you will need to get your muscles accustomed to the strains of cycling and build aerobic fitness – training your heart and lungs to transport more oxygen and your muscles to use it more efficiently.

The key to training is stressing your body then allowing it to recover before stressing it again. Recovery is very important. Slogging away day after day will do you more harm than good.

The great thing when you start is discovering how little you have to do to get results. Remember you won't notice huge benefits at once so, to keep yourself going, measure your progress every month.

Dave Smith, the *MTB Pro* fitness guru, says ride up a long tarmac hill at a set speed, say 12mph. Stop at the top and take a heart rate reading (either using a heart rate monitor or simply by taking your pulse). Use the same hill and the same speed every month and you will see how your heart rate changes as you get fitter. It should drop!

Starting from scratch

You can start to build fitness with as little as three 30-minute rides a week – and you'll want to do more than that anyway. Increase your time by 10 per cent every week for three weeks and just ride for 80 per cent of the third week's time in the fourth week.

Now start again, riding the same times but faster, covering 10 per cent more distance for three weeks and in the fourth doing 80 per cent...

Regular training and rest, gradually increased, will see you well on the way to basic fitness.

Justin will deal with more advanced, race-specific training in Chapter 6, but this will get you enjoying your riding.

Strengths and weaknesses

As you do more riding you'll start to discover what you're good at and

When you want to, you can just take off and be on your own. Just you, the bike, the hills and the sweat burning in your eyes.

LIGHTER IS FASTER!

Skidmarks are a badge of shame behind a real mountain biker. People carve up the countryside because they don't know how to ride, or are riding in the wrong places at the wrong time. When you know how to ride you can pass over the terrain so lightly no one can tell you've been.

Watching top racers is a revelation. They seem to float over the ground avoiding as many obstructions as they can because hitting things slows you down and might damage your bike.

Riding light isn't just earth friendly, it's faster too.

Riders like Volvo Cannondale's Tinker Juarez know that lighter is faster and skids are for kids.

what you're not. It's human nature to do more of what you enjoy, but the human drive is to improve. So draw up a table of the various elements you will encounter on a ride and assess yourself honestly, good, bad or satisfactory.

Your aim is to train out your weaknesses whilst building on your strengths. Don't ignore what you're good at, training should be as enjoyable as possible, otherwise you'll soon get sick of it.

Dave reckons you should spend 50 per cent of your weekly training time on your weaknesses, 20 per cent on your strengths, and the remaining 30 per cent on everything else. This should result in all round improvement and go a long way towards eliminating your failings.

Serious training can absorb tremendous amounts of time, but you don't have to do mega miles to stay reasonably fit. Regular miles and recovery will keep you at a level from which you can quickly improve for a special effort, like a race or a big ride in the high hills. Simply riding to work or college, a minimum of thirty minutes, is a good way of putting in extra miles and maximising your available time.

Building fitness off the bike

Gym work and turbo training are the mountain biker's usual off-bike stand-bys, and a session of swimming once a week will provide a change of scene and excellent relevant exercise.

Upper body strength is important to all of us, and downhillers and trick riders in particular. It's best improved in the gym, again with a structured programme. Tell the instructor what you want to improve and stick to the routine. Don't expect miracles overnight. You probably won't realise how much good it is doing you until you sit down one Sunday night, many weeks later, and wonder why you don't ache after rides any more.

Turbo training is reserved by most folk for winter sessions in the garage, but it is also the most easily controlled and consistent system available. It is especially useful when it is windy, and is a lot safer then riding in the dark. Again, a structured programme is essential and a heart rate monitor will ensure maximum efficiency of training.

SELF-SUFFICIENCY

Self-sufficiency is central to mountain biking. You, or better still, your group, must be properly prepared to complete your ride safely without outside assistance. It's an essential part of being a mountain biker – which is why star racers on huge salaries have to fix their own mechanical problems using equipment and spares they carry with them.

Anyone can have an accident – mechanical failure, injury, getting lost – the important thing is to have planned for those possibilities. Self-sufficiency requires knowledge, planning, self-discipline and guts.

All this might sound over the top in the context of the short rides close to civilisation which is where we all start, but good practice is a lot to do with habit so it makes sense to get into the groove from the start.

Your bike

■ Learn to maintain the bike yourself; regular maintenance and replacement of worn parts saves you those long walks home.
■ Build up a saddle-bag toolkit (see Chapter 5) and carry it with you all

the time. Include a spare inner tube – you can get very cold mending a puncture if the weather turns against you.

Your route

■ Know what the route entails, how long it should take you and how long it might take you. If you're going into the wilds, tell someone where you're heading and when you should be back.
■ Ride within your limits. If you have conducted a genuine self assessment you will have a good idea of your strengths, weaknesses and fitness, and this coupled to knowledge gained on previous outings will give you a good idea of how you will perform on what you are about to undertake.

Don't go mad to start with, plan a route of eight or ten miles (12 or 16km) maximum, and build from there. Your limits will expand naturally, both in distance and severity.

■ Get a weather forecast, but be prepared for the worst.

You

■ You're not going to believe how much food you will eat when you're riding hard! What you take depends on how long you're going to be out, of course, but always take emergency rations – nuts and raisins, mint cake, energy bars, something that will not deteriorate and can be left in your bumbag for weeks at a time. If something breaks, you could be out there much longer than you think.
■ You'll need lots of water too. Whether you carry it in bottles or a Camelbak, top them up wherever you find safe water. I'm afraid even the highest springs and streams aren't necessarily safe to drink from.
■ Dress for the worst of the weather forecast. You get hot riding but cool down quickly when you stop. Layering your clothing is the answer. A sweat-wicking top, a medium weight fleece and a waterproof is a sensible benchmark combination. I always carry a shell waterproof, this is Britain. Clothing is covered in more detail in Chapter 5.

Basic technique

Riding a mountain bike isn't like riding any other sort of bike. Here are some basic principles to get you started:
■ Get out of the saddle. You're going to spend most of your time standing

If you are serious about being a fitter rider then some indoor training workouts are just the ticket.

Once your fitness is sorted, it's time to concentrate on technique.

Descend with your cranks level, head up, bum over the back of the saddle and your arms and legs bent ready to take the bumps.

Corner with your weight on the outside crank, which should be in the six o'clock position.

on the pedals using your weight to combat the terrain. Try it on a bit of rough ground. Get the cranks parallel to the ground, stand on them with your arms and legs relaxed so they act like springs and let the bike move under you. It'll find its way through most things if you let it.

■ Get your weight back on steep downhills. I mean really get it back. On real verts you'll have your bum over the back wheel to keep your centre of gravity in the right place. You'll find it harder to control the bike with your arms locked straight so try to stand up and back with a bit of slack in the arms for control.

■ Get your pedal out of the way in fast corners. You need your inside pedal up away from the ground. The best way is to push the outside pedal right down, stand on it and lean the bike into the corner more than you lean yourself. It keeps the tyres biting. (See Chapter 8)

■ Hunker down on hills. When you start, you're better off sitting in the saddle to climb and spreading your weight between the wheels. Get down low and keep weight on the back wheel for traction and on the front to keep it on the ground. Pedal smoothly. Boot it and the back wheel will spin

and lose its grip.

■ Unweight the wheel that's going to hit. If your front wheel's heading for a rock or the kerb, get your weight back so it hits as light as possible. Then get your weight forward to unweight the back wheel before it hits. You'll learn to actually lift your wheels over obstacles in time (the bunny-hop) but this will do for now.

■ Pedal circles. Toe-clips or clipless pedals help you turn the pedals all the way around, rather than just stomping down. Smooth power through a gear you can pedal easily is less tiring and does less damage than big power peaks. It also keeps the tyres in traction. If they spin, you're not going anywhere.

Go do it

That's about all the information you need for now. There's lot more to come in this book, but you're not going to be able to use it until you've done a bit of riding and developed a feeling for your bike.

So I suggest you just go do it. Now.

CHAPTER 4

transport &delight

COMMUTING, EASY RIDING,

WHAT'S DIFFERENT FOR WOMEN,

TEACHING KIDS TO RIDE

Yes, the mountain bike really is an appropriate, healthy, low cost, quiet, efficient form of individual transport, requiring little oil, no clean air legislation or speed limits (most of the time). And it doesn't kill hedgehogs!

As Tym said in Chapter 1, using your bike on your regular trips over tarmac benefits everyone. Especially you.

The mountain bike design is best for commuting. The semi-upright riding position and indexed gears are ideal in traffic, the fat tyres and tough rims will absorb just about anything that the urban road can throw at you, and cantilever brakes provide loads of stopping power.

And, when the traffic is densest or if there's some sort of jam, you can simply become a pedestrian in an instant and take immediate advantage of their facilities too.

Plus the mountain bike saves you loads of money. Just think of all the dosh you can save on bus or train fares, petrol and parking fees. This saving will pay for your bike in a year or so, and from there on in you're in profit!

SO WHY DON'T MORE PEOPLE DO IT?

The downside

It's a sweaty activity. If you're going to work or college, you need either showers or good washing facilities at your destination, and a change of clothes too.

This may not be such a big problem. A lot of employers have tumbled to the fact that they get more out of fit employees and if these things don't exist you could well find them less reluctant to provide them than you might think.

See if they'll provide lockers too so you can leave some clothes there and not have to carry them in every day.

Bikes get pinched. No point pretending, mountain bikes are attractive to scuzzball thieves. Again, it may not be a problem. There's always secure

BIKE SECURITY

✿ **A good quality U-lock is the only one worth using if you're leaving an attractive bike for any length of time. The smaller the shackle the less vulnerable the U-lock, but it's harder to find things to lock the bike to. Cable locks and chains are pretty much useless.**

✿ **Lock it to something secure. Sounds obvious, but people go on locking bikes to things that can be easily cut or lifted out of the ground.**

✿ **Fill the U-lock. The less room thieves have to apply leverage, the harder it is for them. Take off your front wheel and put the lock around that too.**

✿ **Position the lock so the key hole is as inaccessible as possible.**

RECOMMENDED LOCKS

In a recent test *MTB Pro* gave top marks to the: Kryptonite 2000, Kryptonite New York, Trelock Titan and Squire Paramount. We found U-locks had greatly improved since a test by *MBUK* a year earlier.

RECOMMENDED

space somewhere in a building. Speak nicely to the caretaker or boiler man for a start.

With the right lock and common sense you can make your bike very difficult to steal, even if you have to leave it outside (see Bike Security left). If you can afford two bikes, one that was good a couple of years ago will do the job and is less attractive to thieves.

Cars. Drivers don't see bikes, don't allow for bikes and cars spray out filthy fumes. At most times in most places, these things are just annoyances, but in dense city traffic you really need to be alert and fit to ride effectively.

Remember, to stay safe on a bike in traffic you have to do motorists' thinking for them.

City survival system

Cyclists are the most vulnerable road users in the city. Even pedestrians stand a better chance because they have the pavements. We are out there mixing it with the lot, so how do you survive?

Survival is dependent upon speed, bike handling skills, local knowledge, being noticed and leaving the others in no doubt about where you are going and what you want to do.

We are bound by the traffic laws, but tricks to bypass traffic jams in the interest of health, less time, less fumes are quite valid.

Riding in traffic can be challenging. It needs new techniques, is always eventful, and the more experience you get, the less likely you are to come to harm.

SURVIVAL SKILLS

Become part of the traffic

When traffic speed allows, take up your space where drivers expect another road user to be. You need a good, well maintained machine to do this – an old, heavy bike will slow you down. Lighter equals nimbler and swifter.

✿ Speed: Go for it. Don't dilly dally. Riding slowly annoys drivers. If they don't need to pass, you will gain respect and be absorbed into the traffic on equal terms. If you can go as fast as the other traffic, or even quicker, it is easier to move from lane to lane. Otherwise the likelihood of drivers slowing to allow you to swap lanes is remote.

✿ Use all your lane: Make yourself as wide as possible. If you travel fast enough you're an honorary car.

✿ Position yourself in the middle of your lane at traffic lights. Don't tempt drivers into squeezing past.

Be very aware. Always assume you haven't been seen by the other road user.

☀ If you sneak up the inside lane make sure the drivers know you are there, don't get caught out by vehicles turning left. No indicator is no guarantee they won't turn left.

☀ Keep out of the gutter – that is where all the debris lies: glass, nails, odd bits from cars... Great puncture potential.

☀ You have a right to ride so don't get trodden underfoot – but if it seems inevitable, opt for Plan B and get out of there!

Anticipation

When you can't keep up with traffic you have to ride more defensively. Anticipate everything that might happen and be prepared to take evasive action.

☀ Look way ahead and register what's happening as an advanced driver would. If you're riding between a stream of traffic and a line of parked cars you're vulnerable to a hastily opened car door and pedestrians walking out between vans. Look for the car that's just parked, look under vehicles for legs and feet, look through windscreens. Be ultra aware.

☀ Look behind you often. If you can't do it without wobbling or crashing into the car in front – learn!

☀ Listen. You can usually hear a vehicle approaching fast from behind, or an impatient motorist revving in a low gear. Prepare to take evasive action.

☀ Make plenty of noise. Shout. Wake up dozy motorists and pedestrians. Make sure that they know you are there. Bells and little horns are virtually useless in very heavy traffic.

☀ Expect cars to come straight out of side streets; expect that, even if they have seen you, they will still come out in front of you – they can and frequently do.

☀ Practise skid-free braking. Sit down, keep your weight on the back wheel.

When the smog and pollution get too much, escape for a breath of fresh air.

Be seen

If you've driven a car in traffic you'll know just how easily you miss seeing a bike, even if you're looking out for them.

☀ Wear something horrendously bright – or ride naked, that'll get you noticed!

☀ Signal clearly. Use all your arm to signal. Wave it about if necessary.

☀ Signal in plenty of time. If a driver is close, get eyeball to eyeball contact, and make sure he knows what you want to do.

☀ Take up your position as early as possible, especially when turning right. It could involve a bit of a sprint, which is doubly exciting if trying to signal at the same time.

☀ Never 'undertake' lorries or buses unless you are certain that they won't move while you're next to them. They can't see you well there and can't hear you shout.

Be polite

It's easy to think the whole breed of drivers is out to get you. They're not (only some of them). So don't get aggressive and sullen. Thank motorists for any courtesy extended to you. And if you make a mistake, say you're sorry if you catch them up at the traffic lights. It all helps.

Dealing with an accident

If you do get knocked off your bike, make sure you're able to claim compensation.

☀ Remain calm and polite. Yes you want to kick someone's head in; no, it won't help.

☀ Note the precise point of impact and mark it if you can. A stone or a piece of masonry will do.

☀ Report the accident to the Police.

☀ Obtain the names and addresses of witnesses. This is most important, the Police will simply 'write off' the accident without independent witnesses.

☀ Note the registration numbers of vehicles involved, including parked motors if they are relevant.

☀ Sketch or photograph the scene. Take special notice of the position of vehicles, skid marks and debris.

Wearing bright coloured clothing will help you to be seen by those drivers who are only really looking out for other cars.

ESSENTIAL COMMUTING KIT

- **HELMET**
- **HIGH VISIBILITY JACKET**
- **BRIGHT TIGHTS OR SHORTS** How about white? You'll get noticed, and could develop a whole new circle of friends from the ballet.
- **LIGHTS**
- **REFLECTORS** The lot! British Standard law conformers, pedal strips front and rear facing, wheel arcs, Sam Browne motorcyclist's belt, Scotchlite, ankle and knee bands and finally a Halo for your helmet if it hasn't already got a generous helping of reflective material. This isn't overkill. Bikes are very hard to see at night.
- **MUDGUARDS** City muck isn't just mud, it can be oily, sticky and corrosive.
- **ANTI POLLUTION MASK** Make sure city cycling is doing you good, not harm. Respro make a Scotchlite version of their City Mask. Apart from being an extra reflective item it makes you look really weird.
- **BELL FOR PEDESTRIANS** You only shout at motorists!
- **CYCLE LOCK** As big and as beefy as you can carry!

CITY BAGS

- A couriers bag is best – big enough to hold a change of clothes along with your sandwiches and your lock.
- Second choice is a rucksack. It can double as a day bag for weekend trips, and you automatically take it with you when you get off the bike.
- An old fashioned saddle bag still comes in handy. They are tough, waterproof, will hold all you need on a day to day basis, and they last – I've had my Carradice for 20 years.
- Panniers are roomy, pretty waterproof, usually adorned with extra reflective material, but you still get your hands dirty taking them off and replacing them for the journey home.

Always assume the next car door is going to open and be prepared to take avoiding action.

⚙ Keep the bike in its damaged state until it has been seen by the Police.

This is a lot to ask when you've just been knocked off your bike, a friend might be able to do it for you and you can do it for another cyclist if the need arises.

A better deal for cyclists

Holland and Sweden are renowned for their thousands of kilometres of cycle paths, Britain is not. There are seven times as many accidents to cyclists in the UK as there are in either of those countries. I rest my case.

Groups campaigning on behalf of cyclists say that just 1 per cent of the cost of the current road building programme could provide magnificent cycle facilities throughout Britain, and probably fill in all the potholes on the existing roads too.

Politicians talk a lot of bike friendly words, but if they did something like this it would have the knock on effect of encouraging more people to use bikes for everyday journeys.

Simple improvements, such as safe storm drain grates with all the ribs at 90 degrees to the kerb, instead of the current bike traps, increased and improved access to bridges and public buildings, and better bike racks would cost little and help a lot.

These facilities exist in other countries, why not here?

If you want to help stir up the authorities and get them to imitate bike friendly cities like York and Edinburgh, join your local cycle action group. There is one in most large cities, your local library will be able to help with contact numbers.

DELIGHT!

A family or a group of friends riding easily through beautiful country doesn't make a particularly exciting picture, but it's what most mountain bikes are used for.

You've no doubt seen amazing stunts and epic adventures in *Mountain Biking UK*, but those stunts take hours to learn and inflict a lot of damage on the bike, and the adventures absorb an awful lot of time. Most of us won't get into that at all but will simply enjoy getting out and about, often into places that we have passed by at a greater speed missing much of interest.

There is no need to kill yourself, mountain biking is all about having pleasure.

And that's what it will be so long as you don't attempt to do too much initially. To make it a pleasure for everyone, ride to the ability of the

A group ride livens up familiar terrain that's normally ridden alone.

weaker member of the group, and choose interesting routes or a destination that has something extra to offer.

The easy routes

As I mention in Chapter 3, the best starter routes are railway or canal paths. Some of these are excellent, not sub standard in any way, and, most important when you have a group of mixed ability, they're flat.

The rock hopping, storm bound brigade rather look down on these routes for that very reason, but they're missing out on some terrific enjoyment. I never tire of them, there is always something new to see in the way of wildlife or industrial archaeology.

If you start from the coast, railway paths often climb gently inland meaning it is downhill all the way back – what more could you want?

Canal paths are not all considered suitable for riding, but those that are

There is enough space for all countryside users to enjoy nature without getting on each others' nerves. Use your head so you can all have fun.

SUSTRANS The railway path people have local contacts all over the country. Head office: 35 King Street, Bristol BS1 4DZ ☎ 0117 926 8893
FOREST ENTERPRISE Most forests now have waymarked routes, but this is an ongoing development. Forest Enterprise are actively promoting these routes. Head Office: 231 Corstorphine Road, Edinburgh, Midlothian EH12 7AT
☎ 0131 334 0303

CANALS
A complete set of cyclist's information sheets for the whole of the British Waterways network is available from British Waterways Consumer Services, Willow Grange, Church Road, Watford WD1 3QA
☎ 01923 226422

CANAL CYCLING

There is no general public right of way for cyclists on towpaths but you may cycle with care along some stretches on some canals, provided you display a valid British Waterways permit on your bicycle and observe their safety code. Some permits are free of charge, available from waterway offices.

In most cases canal routes are not continuous, it is necessary to use local byways to connect the ridable stretches. Having said that, there's miles of easy, enjoyable riding out there.

open to bikes are well worth a visit. You must get a permit from British Waterways, but that is no problem. Waterfowl are usually the star attraction, invariably trying to share your sandwiches.

Sharing the trails

Most cycle paths, railway paths and towpaths are shared facilities, in other words also used by pedestrians and occasionally horses. Don't spoil any one else's day. Who's in a hurry anyway?

Remember how quiet bikes can be! Don't sneak up on other users, slide silently by twenty centimetres from their shoulders and frighten the wits out of them. Give a ding on your bell or a polite "Good morning" from some distance away.

Give people time to react to your approach, to bring the dog to heel or get the nag under control.

Remember horses are temperamental animals and may spook at anything – a bunch of brightly coloured mountain bikers appearing suddenly is definitely 'anything'. It makes sense to stop and get off the track to let horses go by. Some horses are not under proper control and any horse can get out of control; they're big and heavy, and you could come off worst. Be very wary.

Pedestrians (and we're all pedestrians a lot of the time) never walk in a straight line! This is especially true of elderly dog lovers. Don't expect them to stay where they are, they're in a world of their own and it's their

You can always get away from the people, the noise and the familiar.

prerogative! It's allowed.

☼ **Yech department:** Railway paths near urban areas are often used as dog lavatories, and there is a good chance of trapping some offensive material in the tread of your tyre. Worse still are the fragments that are not trapped! Mudguards help a lot, Crud Guards are even better!

A bit wilder

If you're travelling specifically to find a good day's riding, try one of the Forest Enterprise set-ups. Over the last few years they have been making forest roads and tracks available to mountain bikers and have done a lot to attract and look after us.

Well marked, mapped routes suited to different abilities are to be found. If you're looking for something harder, remember a lot of British races use these trails, there are challenges if that's what you're looking for.

Wilder still

Be reasonable in your early ambitions. Yes, I've said it before, but seriously, you could put yourself off for life by over exertion, not to mention your long-suffering family and friends.

For example, don't put the bike on the back of the car and head for the Lake District, Scotland or Wales unless you are already super fit.

Or, if you must, choose a route that will take you deep into the big hills without actually climbing them. Here are a couple:

Ennerdale: A great starter in the Lakes; you can ride miles up to Black Sail youth hostel on reasonable forest road without any lung bursting climbs until the latter stages.

Celtic forests: There are great waymarked mountain bike routes to suit all abilities in the Border Forests of the Upper Tweed near Peebles, and many of the Welsh forests offer miles of roads that will take you deep into the mountains. Forest roads are a great way to get away from it all without killing yourself. Try some.

TRANSPORTING YOUR BIKES

Getting to the ideal family rides often means transporting the bikes by car.

What's the best method?

There are nearly as many different types and makes of racks for carrying them as there are mountain bikes.

The safest and most secure way of transporting a bike is to put it inside the car, but even if you run a battleship (like my Ford Granada Estate), there won't be much room for four people. If you dismantle a bike it will fit inside virtually any vehicle, but this is not always convenient, and eventually damages the upholstery. Most people sling them on the outside using some kind of rack.

If you're bored with the local stuff, it's time to pop the bikes on to the car and take a drive to explore a new area.

There are three basic designs of rack: roof racks, which are bars which sit in the vehicle gutters, fitted with clamps for saddle and front forks; rear racks which sit on the boot or hatchback secured by a system of straps; or towbar mounted racks which make use of the stout fitting (usually) already provided for some other purpose.

They all have their advantages and disadvantages.

Roof racks: They're the cheapest, that's the advantage. The twin disadvantages are height and invisibility. A bike on the roof of the car is exposed to the winds, so much so you may lose it off the top – it'll certainly slow you down and up your fuel consumption. You're also likely to knock it off the top attempting to go beneath one of those anti-caravette barriers that restrict access to some Lakeland car parks... You can't see it, so you don't know what it's doing.

Rear mounted racks: These have the advantage that you have the bike in sight at all times, but the slight disadvantage is that the bike obscures your rearward vision to some degree, and may also obscure your registration plate and indicators too. The great advantage of these racks is that they are usually slung low, virtually out of the wind, and allow you to go quicker. I used one for for eight years.

Towbar mounted racks: Expensive, but highly recommended for greater security in transit and ease of stowage. They have the advantage of keeping the bike well clear of the vehicle paintwork, but the disadvantage of cost. If you fit a towbar to accept the baseplates for this sort of rack, have the appropriate electrics installed at the same time, and buy a

If day trips aren't enough of a challenge, break out the rucksacks. Overleaf – Make the most of every second. You'll be back to reality soon enough.

lighting board with all the legal trappings, you can spend the best part of £200. The result is great. The rack is rock solid, fireproof, legal, and you've the rain to wash the worst of the mud off on the way home.

Rackcraft

Don't skimp on fastenings: Elastic bungees will attach to just about anything – towing eyes, hinges, the rack itself.

Car care: Fasten pedals so they can't revolve and scratch the paintwork. Stick transparent Fablon or Contac to areas where the securing straps, feet or bungees run over the bodywork, and renew from time to time. Do the same to the rear windscreen if the feet are prone to touching the glass.

Fit an isolator switch to the rear windscreen wiper. Inadvertent activation could burn out the motor if the wiper cannot complete a full cycle.

Plumber's pipe lagging will protect bike frames when two or more are carried.

WOMEN AND MOUNTAIN BIKES

There are plenty of super fit women riders, and I have my legs torn off regularly by a couple of them to prove it. But it's a fact that most women come to mountain bikes through their men. It's also a fact that family and sociable friendly rides are much better with women about.

In most cases the woman will be the newest to riding, getting used to the equipment, still getting fit and not as strong as the men. Once over the initial hurdles with skills to compensate for lack of upper body strength, women get hooked as powerfully as men. But only if they have the right equipment, correctly set up, and get proper support in the early stages. Most women are put off mountain biking by the male ego which simply cannot resist charging off down ridiculous trails leaving them struggling off the back. So, men, if you don't want women around, that's what you do. But it's your loss.

Women: don't put up with it! Tell 'em!

Here's what you need to bear in mind when buying your equipment:

✪ Bikes: Most mountain bikes are made for men. They need adjusting to suit women. Forget women's frames, though, they simply aren't strong enough for real off-road use.

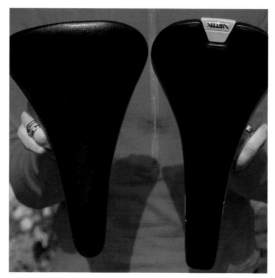

Sore bits are no fun. Buy a saddle that fits YOU not your pocket.

✪ The frame must fit you, of course, but bear in mind that like most women, you are probably shorter in the arms than a man of the same height and need a shorter top tube. See Brant's bike set-up advice in Chapter 2. Try out different models if you can because the geometry can vary enormously. A slightly smaller frame and longer seat tube might be the answer. If that fails, the magazines carry advertisements for specialists in women's frames.

✪ Get yourself a woman's saddle. This is absolutely crucial. Most saddles are made for men, but the female pelvic bones are wider apart. If they're too wide to be supported by the saddle, the genital area takes a terrible pounding.

All riders get saddle sore and you might imagine the pain you're suffering is normal and put up with it. It's not, so don't. There are plenty of specialist women's saddles around which are broader in the seat and shorter in the nose. The Terry range is the favourite of serious women riders.

All new riders benefit if their companions ride at their pace. But men enjoy testing each other out and simply love showing off to women. It's just thoughtlessness. If they leave you gasping, yell at them a bit. They'll soon find riding slower is a different sort of pleasure and might even be glad of the excuse.

You don't have to ride like a man (unless you want to). Upper body strength is essential on really rough terrain and it'll be hard work for most of you. Even the toughest women riders tend to choose a different line from the men, avoiding the worst of the boulders. They make up for the lack of strength with skill and delicately ride over and through sections where I would have no hesitation in dismounting.

Tandems

Tandems are the relationship saver! When two partners are of very different ability, with one having to wait and the other feeling like they have to speed up all the time – but they still want to ride together off-road – this is the answer. Off-road tandem riding is a totally different discipline and one of the most exciting things you can ever do. However, you do need to be a fully competent solo rider before even attempting it, but if you're into laughter, panic, technicality and speed all at the same time, do it. They are fantastic!

With a comfy seat attached you can spend all day in the saddle.

KIDS AND MOUNTAIN BIKES

Children love riding bikes, but the roads aren't kid-friendly. Riding off-road is sheer pleasure for them and for the adult in charge of them (unless you try to take them too far and end up carrying the bikes!).

Let's start at the very beginning – teaching kids to ride. There are all sorts of aids which are supposed to help, but you can't teach balance by making it unnecessary. The best method, I regret to tell you, is on a flat surface with an adult, bent double, running along behind, holding the saddle. It's quick and it's painful (but only to the adult).

They'll need a bit of riding on the tarmac before they've got the skills and stamina to ride off-road, but here are four important things to consider when you reckon they're ready for a mountain bike:

■ Everyone needs a bike that fits, including kids. Yes, they grow fast, but while they're 'growing into' a bike that's too big they can hurt themselves – these are young bodies, look after them.

If you buy a reasonable bike it will have a resale value in a year or two's time. Accept the loss for the sake of your child's comfort and enjoyment.

■ Brake levers. Look for a reach adjustment screw at the lever when you buy a bike, children's hands are a lot smaller than ours. Kids bikes should have this adjustment.

■ Gear levers should be easy for a small hand to operate. This is very hard to find on kids bikes, although the equipment does exist and it's something that's worth having changed at the shop.

■ We all wear helmets, including kids. Insist! If a cool helmet is considered a fashion accessory, it's unlikely to be a problem.

There are plenty of mountain bikes specially designed for kids, so do them a favour and get them riding off-road.

Getting the bike right

Whether you buy new or second-hand, check the bike over mechanically before you start them on it.

Brakes: See that the blocks are correctly aligned on the rims, that they can reach the levers and that these are in line with the arms so the wrists don't have to be cocked to use them. With everything so big, aching hands are a common problem.

Wheels: Make sure the wheelnuts or quick releases are tight.

Tyres: Don't blow the tyres up too hard; about 40lbs will be ample.

Gears: Make sure they function correctly. They will never learn to use them if they don't work. Younger kids, up to around seven, are so light

they may only need five or six gears.

Riding position: Lower the saddle a little in the very early stages to give extra confidence. Make sure their feet can reach the ground!

Handlebars: Ensure they can reach the handlebars comfortably. Raise them if necessary.

Basic riding technique

Good basic riding should be taught from the outset. It's just as relevant to novice adults too. Here's what to teach them:

Starting off

■ Change into a lower gear before coming to a halt. This will make starting off again that much easier.

■ Always start off with the same foot. This will soon become a natural routine.

■ Get the starting foot on to the pedal, and the pedal half way down the power stroke, then there isn't too much strength required.

■ Hold the bike steady against the brakes, check for obstructions in your path.

■ All clear? Pull on the handlebar, press on that pedal and you're off.

■ Start sitting down to keep the centre of gravity as low as possible.

Stopping

■ Decide which foot you are going to put down before you stop. It is much easier to use the uphill foot on rough ground.

■ Turn into the hill just before you stop. This changes the angle of the bike, takes the weight off the handlebar and makes it easier to put your foot down.

■ Keep your feet on the pedals until just before you come to a stop. This maintains weight on the front wheel for steering. No hopping or you'll break your ankle.

■ Use both brakes. On long, steep hills brake early to avoid skidding and losing control.

Climbing

■ Mentally divide the hill into stages, each bit an attainable challenge.

■ Be determined to ride to the top.

■ Stay in the saddle. Stand up only for very short stretches.

■ Choose the best line. Parents may have to lead.

■ Stay in the saddle when tyres really need to grip.

C H A P T E R   5

touring
& expeditions

PREPARING FOR EXPEDITIONS,

CLOTHING, NAVIGATION,

UK ADVENTURE, RIDING ABROAD

If the *MBUK* pictures that thrill you most show mountain bikers hacking their way into the Scottish wilderness, assaulting the High Andes or gritting across the Sahara, you're absolutely right!

There's nothing to beat the feeling of achievement, excitement and sheer enjoyment you get from being self-sufficient in the wilderness.

Of course you might be looking at those pictures and thinking 'that would be great to do, but I'm not really up to it'.

Well, I'm here to tell you you can do it, probably not next weekend, perhaps even not this year, but if you build up to it anything is possible. You already have the key: the interest and a mountain bike.

The build-up
If you've never done anything like this before, begin with a six mile (ten kilometre) ride to a pub lunch or a picnic, then the same back. I prefer picnics because you can stop where you fancy, no time is wasted waiting for service, and you're off again. Next week do the same, but off-road; it will take longer but it will be more of an adventure. Gradually pub lunches will become a thing of the past, you'll start brewing up in the lee of dry

stone walls and become expert in the art of dining al fresco.

The next step is extending the duration of the rides; the mileage is irrelevant, it's the time that counts. By doing it regularly you will build fitness and become used to navigating through unfamiliar countryside. Inevitably there will be mistakes, mini-disasters, long rides home after map reading errors, but this is all part of the fun. In fact these are the days that will linger in the memory.

Do it on long summer days when a couple of hours extra shouldn't be too much of a disaster; short winter days are not the time to be extending yourself.

Multi-day rides
Most of you are probably well into day rides already. That's where a lot of people get stuck. Again you can build up to multi-day rides gradually.

Stringing together day rides by using B&B accommodation is the next

People who travel extended distances by mountain bike are a particular breed. Until you try you'll never know if you can hack it.

step. This eliminates the need to retrace your route, you get into new countryside, you learn how to feed yourself for 24 hours, and you become used to carrying more luggage. Extra kit always alters the handling of the bike, so get used to it as soon as you can. Once you've had a few two-day forays you can launch into a full British tour.

UK tours

Planning and following a route through the sort of country that turns you on can be attacked three different ways. The easiest is to plan it around B&B, youth hostel or camping barn accommodation. Which you choose will be dictated by your budget.

The second option is the base camp approach. You pitch your tent somewhere central to the riding area and ride out from there. It's ideal for family or group adventures. A base camp has the advantage that most of the kit can be left behind, allowing you to ride light and possibly farther, but of course you need to return to the same place each night until you motor on and relocate to explore another area.

The great step forward is that you get used to living in a tent. And it takes some practice! For many people camping is a full time job. Cooking, eating, washing devours all their time. Try to break camp from waking to getting rolling in two hours – it is astonishing where the time goes. The secret of quick camping is to take note of the items that are NOT used and leave them behind next time. Hone your camping to its lightweight limits before starting to camp out in the wilds.

Before you know it you will have drifted into full blown UK expeditions, carrying all your kit, food, sleeping bag and mat. This is the third option, the most flexible, and the hardest work. But, despite all this talk of wilderness, you are never too far away from civilisation in the shape of roads in the UK. Shops can be few and far between, but in all fairness, even if crossing Scotland by the most mountainous route you won't need food for more than 24 hours, unless a Sunday is included.

Surviving in the wild

Once you start carrying all your kit with you on the bike you'll become very weight conscious. You'll discover why we pay so much for ultra-light outdoor kit. Big sleeping bags will be replaced by lighter, more expensive models; cooking utensils trimmed to a minimum; forks will disappear and the spoon becomes universal – with a sharp edge filed on to it. Clothing becomes multi-purpose, and those net pockets on the sides of rucksacks and panniers become life savers, drying your clothing as you ride along.

So what do you need to survive? And how do you carry all this gear?

Again there are three ways of doing it: carry it all on your bike, all on yourself in a rucksack, or combine the two.

It pays to be the hardy, cheerful type whenever the weather decides to play its joker.

SADDLE PACK CONTENTS

These are the actual contents of my own day to day bag
- ✿ Spare inner tube
- ✿ Tyre levers
- ✿ Tools:
  Selection of appropriate allen keys
  Small adjustable spanner
  Chain splitter
  Small screwdriver – for gear mechs
  Small pair of pliers
- ✿ Piece of soft copper wire – to tie back

broken bits!
- ✿ Puncture repair outfit – with two 5mm screws and Nylok nuts in the box for loose racks
- ✿ Mini First Aid kit – Boots special, plasters, wipes, even scissors
- ✿ Roll of narrow micropore tape – mends specs and tyre splits too!
- ✿ Space blanket or bivvy bag
- ✿ Polaris Switchback shell jacket – honest, this does live there!

Developing a taste for cuisine al fresco is all part of touring by bike.

Overleaf - What you lose in travel comfort you gain in adrenalin and views.

Unless you are going somewhere very hot, the last option is best. Consider the following, and build up your luggage wardrobe accordingly.

For all rides

Tool bag: The easiest way to carry tools is in a little saddle pack tied under the seat. There is a huge choice, but those with Velcro fastenings are most convenient to use. Another option is a frame fitting triangular bag that doubles as shoulder padding for carries.

For overnight stops

Bumbags: The expanding type with two compartments is favourite; it has the advantage that your back will get plenty of air when the top section is tucked away. If you need more room, add a bar bag. Not to keep your camera in, though, although many come compartmentalised for cameras. There is a lot of vibration at the handlebar, my preference is a tailor made padded CCS (Camera Care Systems) case worn like a bumbag, or stuffed in the top section of the Karrimor Redwood expander.

Rucksacks: Obviously rucksacks are bigger, so you can get more in them, but don't go mad and buy a giant. You've got to carry the thing on your back, and this can be quite a challenge when riding off-road.

Go for design not size. My faithful Karrimor KIMM Sac has six pockets in addition to the main compartment, giving a 30 litre capacity, which is sufficient. There are three net pouch pockets around the base and a large zipped net pocket on the lid.

It will take a few trips to learn how much you feel comfortable touring with. Avoid overloading, which can be more of a pain than having too little.

Remember the value of net for drying gear as you ride along. There are two excellent zipped pockets built into the padded waist strap, ideal for the first aid kit, whistle and wallet. The whole ensemble can be tensioned into a solid unit by the zig zag cords. There is also a lightweight chest strap, positioned high enough for women to use too, which puts the final touch to a very secure pack.

It is absolutely paramount that your rucksack becomes part of you for comfortable days out in the hills. If it doesn't your bike handling will suffer and most of the enjoyment disappear.

Going wilder

The rack: If you are going wilder you'll need a rack to carry the tent and sleeping mat. A rack is the most streamlined way to carry it. Mats don't weigh much but produce horrendous wind resistance if carried atop the rucksack. Roll it around the tent and strap them down well along the rack.

For longer expeditions there are all sorts of pannier and bag combinations, but concentrate on keeping your load down. Two of you, with judicious load sharing and a clever choice of kit, could keep the weight down to 5.5kg (12lbs) each, Polaris Challenge style.

CLOTHING

The layering principle: You work hard on a bike, you sweat, you struggle uphill at slow speed, then freefall down the other in a blast of cold air. The only way to keep your body dry and neither too hot nor too cold is to layer your clothing.

Base layer: Next to your skin you need garments which wick moisture away, keeping you dry and warm. You'll still sweat when working hard but the garment will dry as you ride if it's made of the right stuff. Polartec, Capilene and Rhovyl are material trade names to look out for. Cotton T-shirts just get sodden and chilly.

Heavy duty: When the weather turns really cold, go for a long sleeved turtle neck, preferably with a zip so you can let the heat out on climbs.

Mid-layer: To maintain the flow of moisture out into the atmosphere the mid-layer needs to be made from a wicking, breathable fabric too. Fleeces do this job admirably. They come in a variety of weights, but a medium fleece is a good starter. Add this to your thermal base layer and you have a very warm combination.

Heavy duty: Open-weave fleeces can let wind and cold air through,

Keep dry and not too hot or cold by layering your clothing.

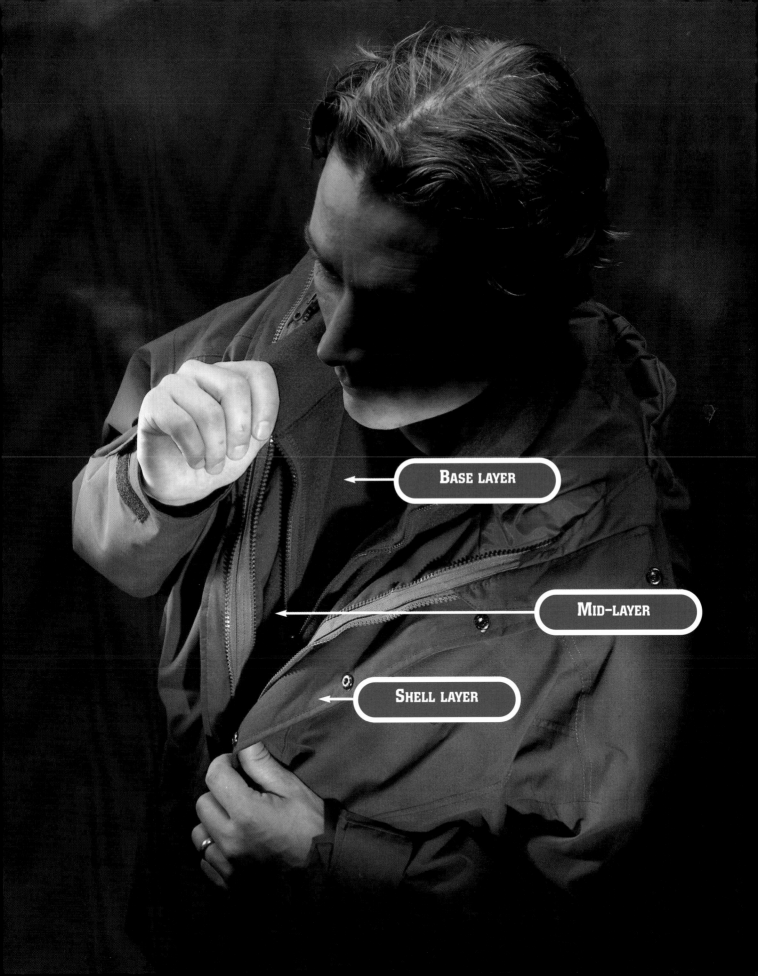

I choose my gear from the following list :

BASE LAYER

North Cape Thermal Zip Turtle
North Cape Long sleeve T top
Karrimor ABL Roll-neck shirt

MID-LAYER

Karrimor Road & Mountain jersey
Karrimor Moab jacket
Calange Snappy
Calange Mountainlite – reversible showerproof

LIGHTWEIGHT SHELL

Polaris Switchback shell
Karrimor Vail Cape

WATERPROOF SHELL

Karrimor Aspen GTX
Polaris Stratum Jacket

BOTTOMS

Karrimor Slick Rock bib tights
Calange Hot Bots
Calange Stretchlites
North Cape Polartec 200 salopettes
Polaris Re-action Pants
Ron Hill Trackster Trek

DEEPEST WINTER

North Cape Ogre Jacket – Polartec 1000
North Cape Ogre Salopant – Polartec 1000

FOOTWEAR

Karrimor KSB 3 GTX

this needs to be breathable too, otherwise you could drown in your own sweat.

There are dozens of garments available on the market, the Gear List left shows what I use.

Winter wardrobe

Even in winter, conditions vary greatly and I tend to swap around a lot depending mainly on how high I am going. The theoretical drop of one degree Celsius for every 150m of height gained doesn't matter so much at the height of summer, but coupled to potential wind chill in winter it can make a lot of difference. Bib tights to eliminate the cold spot on your back are worth their weight in gold, and don't forget your hands, head and feet.

Summer wardrobe

There is no great difference. Simply wear less. The base layer will double as a T-shirt, obviously you will discard the bib tights, and normal mountain bike shoes or boots will replace the KSBs. You may still require the heaviest waterproof!

DEALING WITH DANGER

Face it, danger is the spur. If there was no risk there would be no challenge and that's more than half the reason most of us love it. I'm not talking about taking risks, any fool can do that, the buzz is overcoming the danger through proper planning, knowledge, endurance and skill.

Accidents, of course, can always happen, although you'll be surprised how carefully you ride when there's fifty miles of inhospitable moor between you and help.

The most likely risk, particularly when you're starting wild riding, is misjudging the task or your ability and getting caught out on the hills at night, lost, cold and lacking protection. More likely in winter, of course, when short days leave little margin for error and error is most dangerous.

The golden rules are:

- ✿ Plan your route thoroughly
- ✿ Estimate how long it will take accurately
- ✿ Tell someone reliable where you are going and when you should be back
- ✿ Plan for possible emergencies

Of these, estimating the time it will take is the most difficult.

Estimating journey time

Mountain biking will take you not only into hilly regions where average times can be affected by climbing and descending, but the actual nature of the terrain cannot be judged from the map, and conditions underfoot

reducing their effectiveness to a huge degree in certain conditions. To combat this some of the latest fleeces have been produced with a very tight weave, others use a breathable but windproof chest panel of Pertex. For really tough conditions there is Polartec 1000, a fleece sandwich with a breathable membrane in the middle. This makes it totally windproof, extremely warm and reasonably waterproof too.

Shell layer: The final requirement for the British weather is a waterproof shell, or at least something that will repulse the worst of the water. Ideally

With properly loaded, well set up bikes you can travel with surprising speed.

can vary immensely. I have been working for years on a system that will give a good, consistent estimate based on what can be gleaned from the map, and finally put it to the test with a group of rookies in the *MBUK* Wilderness Masterclass last year.

It works pretty well over a long ride, although mechanicals, accidents and vicious terrain can put estimates for shorter legs wildly out.

It's based on the following average speeds and times:

Tarmac @ 10mph = 6 minutes per mile
Bridleway @ 5mph = 12 minutes per mile
Rough moor @ 3mph = 20 minutes per mile

Here's how estimates based on these figures worked out for real:

Phase 1 tarmac – estimate 24 minutes
Variable 1: The tarmac was steeply uphill, it climbed 252m in the first 4.3 miles, 0.22 miles further than the estimate measured off the map.
Variable 2: There was a puncture. Then the tyre split, then the spare tube also had a puncture.
Result: We lost 32 minutes in the first four miles!

Phase 2 bridleway – estimate 11 minutes
Started badly, the much repaired tyre went flat, the pump broke!
Result: Another 6 minutes were lost.

Phase 3 bridleway/moor – estimate 23 minutes
Variable 1: The bridleway crossed tussocky moorland, where we knew it would be tough, but things went well despite the struggle.
Result: We only lost a minute and a half.

Phase 4 moorland – estimate 17 minutes
Variable: There was no real track on the ground.
This phase didn't go well. There was a bit of a dispute where the best path lay, the truth being there is no track at all, only a few impressions made by the deer, goats and the odd wandering sheep.
Result: There was a loss of another 4 minutes.

Phase 5 bridleway – estimate 38 minutes
This was a bridleway superimposed upon a forest road, and steeply downhill. We could probably have clawed back all the lost time with a session of wacky descending, but we were tired after the bog flog and weren't about to throw caution to the wind.
Result: We ended up amazingly only 17 minutes adrift from the original estimate. Not bad all things considered. Try it for yourselves. Match the speeds to your own performance, and get to know how accurately you can estimate a route.

ACCIDENTS

Whether you are turning out for an hour in the evening or undertaking a long distance adventure, you cannot afford to have accidents. The big objective is to complete the challenge with a minimum of distractions. Getting killed can spoil your day!

Careful planning can reduce the risk of accidents, careful riding can virtually eliminate them, but they do occur. There is no need to approach every trip in an atmosphere of gloom, but if you accept there is always the possibility of an accident, you can allow for it at the planning stage.

Escape routes: When planning your route for the day, always mark the nearest sources of help and how to get there. Never skimp on maps, get the most detailed and accurate there are (harder when travelling abroad, often you can't get the best maps until you're there).

Injury: Decide in advance what you will do in case of serious injury – how many will stay with the casualty, how many will go for help. Don't leave that decision until panic has set in.

It is best for two people to go for help, in case one has a further accident. Parties of four are ideal for assaults on the big stuff.

Medical supplies: Check you have the first aid kit before setting off, it usually provokes hilarity but acts as a gentle reminder.

First Aid

My advice to any group of serious riders is simple: go on a first aid course – all of you. A specialist first aider is not much use if he's unconscious. And if you break a limb it may be possible for you to direct operations, so you know they're doing it right! (It happened to me.)

Seriously, if the opportunity to do a course arises at college or work, take it, you never know when it will come in handy, and it's a useful qualification if you want to do something in the outdoors field.

Going for help

Next to the mobile phone, the mountain bike is the fastest means of summoning help in the hills, because it is invariably downhill to the telephone. But, and it is a HUGE but, don't get over excited and wipe out on the way down, be reasonable. You are no use to anyone if you are lying in a crumpled heap.

Fuel up, keep rolling

All your plans go to hell if one of the party falls by the wayside. One of the most common reasons for 'bonking' (running out of energy) is a failure to eat and drink properly. Take food at regular intervals, either nibbling as you ride, or stopping for breaks every two or three hours. It is so easy to forget to eat and drink, especially in winter when you don't sweat so much, but you still lose fluids exhaling breath and this must be replaced by sipping or drinking.

Emergency rations must always be carried, in fact they should be part of your bumbag kit. Long lasting bars include mint cake, PowerBars and Mars bars.

NAVIGATION

There is a lot of snobby technical talk about navigation, and compass use in particular, and it's enough to put a lot of riders off ever attempting to use one. Unless you go very remote, get lost in the dark or caught high on the hill in dense cloud on a regular basis you will probably never need one, but navigation is a skill every complete mountain biker should have.

We navigate every day without thinking about it, making our way to college, work and then home again. You never need a compass for that. For day rides you draw a route on the map and follow it successfully on most occasions. If you pay attention to where you are going, and your surroundings you shouldn't get lost so long as you:

Get a good map. In this country this means an Ordnance Survey map,

If you want to avoid getting lost in the fog you should learn basic map reading skills (TIP: learn them BEFORE you get lost).

Supported tours mean that you don't have to lug all your own gear, and can even give up and ride in the jeep if the hills get too much.

either 1:50,000 Landranger or 1:25,000 Pathfinder. Learn what the symbols mean, they differ between the Landranger and Pathfinder! You will find the most important in Chapter 3.

Use it. Most of the tracks we use are well defined, bridleways, Landrover or grouse moor roads, so they are relatively easy to follow. However, if the way shrinks to a narrow sheep track, check the map! It may still be correct, there are thousands of bridleways that are no more than a skinny path through the heather, but check just the same and confirm your position.

Look for signs. It is amazing where you find signposts to confirm the route. Most county councils in England and Wales have a Rights of Way Department which sees to the signposting, while the Scottish Rights of Way Society do it north of the Border. You will find their fingerposts at track junctions even in the depths of the Highlands.

Basic compass technique

I shan't attempt to cover the subject in depth here, but this description of basic technique should convince you how easy it is:

Baseplate type compasses, like those made by Suunto and Silva, are easiest to use. The three most important features of these instruments are the edge of the baseplate, which is used to join points on the map, the rotating capsule which houses the magnetic needle, and the direction of travel arrow, usually etched into the centre of the baseplate, which will point the way for you.

Step 1: Orientate the map so the north edge (top), points North. (Do it with one hand, holding the compass with your thumb. That way you keep the map and the compass together while using your other hand to swivel the compass).

Turn both the compass and the map until the grid lines and the red end of the compass needle point North.

(There is a slight complication here in that grid North differs from magnetic North by about 5°, but you can allow for that when you become more competent.)

Step 2: Keeping the map in this position, place the compass on the map with the edge along your desired line of travel. Rotate the capsule again until the 'N' on the compass bezel (the outer movable ring) points to magnetic North on the map, more or less aligned with the grid lines.

Step 3: Pick up the compass and turn your whole body around until the compass needle points to the 'N' on the bezel. The 'Direction of Travel' arrow in the baseplate now points precisely to your destination.

Step 4: Pick out a landmark and ride towards it.

When you reach that landmark, use the compass again, pick another

1 Orienteering arrow

2 Graduated movable bezel

3 Scale

4 Magnifying lens

5 Romer for grid reference

6 Hole for carrying cord

7 Compass housing

8 Orientating lines

9 Compass needle, North end red

10 Baseplate

11 Direction of travel arrow

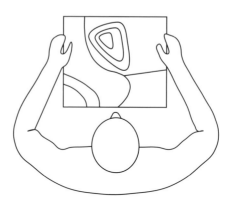

Note that the map is set in relation to the ground and will always lie along the same axis regardless of the direction travelled.

TRAVELLING NORTH

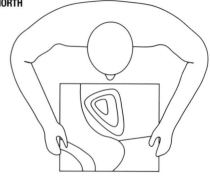

TRAVELLING SOUTH

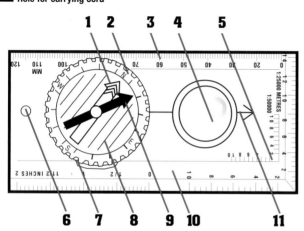

1 2   3   4   5

6   7   8   9 10   11

Look for landmarks to check your position with the map.

and ride on. Roads and tracks seldom follow a straight course so the landmark system is the easiest.

Once you get back on to the right track you can resume navigating by observation.

That's all there is to it.

• Navigation is a big subject and fascinating in itself. If you want to find out more, read *Advanced Mountain Biking* by Derek Purdy. He's too modest to plug it himself, but I can! Ed

Cycle computers

Mountain bikers have a huge advantage over others in the hills because, if your cycle computer is calibrated correctly, you will know exactly how far you have travelled.

Make a route card by measuring the distances off the map before you set off, trip the computer at each junction or feature listed, and you'll probably never need the compass (that doesn't mean you should leave it at home though).

Cycle computers can help keep you on the right track and gauge your progress.

EXPEDITIONS ABROAD

Taking your bike abroad introduces new heights of adventure, whether you go absolutely mad and choose somewhere right off the beaten track or, more sensibly for the first time, pick somewhere fairly civilised. Either way adventure will in no way be diminished because you'll be in totally new territory, you will need to find your way about, the people will talk funny, there could be a different attitude to cyclists and you might find they see very few mountain bikes.

One of the great things about mountain bikes is that they're usually dead cheap to transport and if you take a tent, you only have to feed yourself – which you have to do anyway.

So how do you get abroad as cheaply as possible?

Ferries

If you're within riding distance of a ferry or can cadge a lift, this is the cheapest way. If there is a convenient mountain biking area at the far end that is even better, although you're more likely to have to spend a day or two getting to the hills.

Once there you may want to establish a base – I always seem to find a brilliant area and stop there, riding every pass and every jeep track in the area. I get great satisfaction from this, knowing a little piece of a far off land intimately. But I have many friends who couldn't stand that and like to keep moving, moving, moving.

Try a bit of both and see which you like best.

The bus

The Cyclists Touring Club in association with Bolero Travel run the European Bike Express. The pick-up route in England starts at Middlesbrough and weaves its way south to Dover, picking up at several points, usually motorway service areas or recognised bus stations.

There are services to France, Spain and Italy, each with several drop off points at the other end. A major attraction is that you can leave the bus at one location and rejoin it for the return journey at another.

Details from European Bike Express, 31 Baker Street, Middlesbrough TS1 2LF ☎ 01642 251440.

Flying

Not half as difficult as you might think, and even easier if you fly from your local airport.

Fly it free: The personal baggage allowance on scheduled flights is usually 30kg, charter flights 20kg. Your bike probably weighs about 13kg, so take it as your baggage allowance and you will still have a little to

When touring abroad you may encounter conditions you just don't get at home. When was the last time you rode through a sandstorm in Essex?

FERRYING YOUR BIKE

Prices are always rising, but the cost of taking a bike is a fraction of the price you pay for your passenger ticket, or even free of charge.

BRITTANY FERRIES . . . . . .All routes FREE, even to Spain

NORTH SEA FERRIES . . . .All routes FREE, and food is included in the price of your ticket!

P & O FERRIES . . . . .All routes FREE, even to Spain

SEACAT . . . . .Folkestone – Boulogne (France) FREE

STENA SEALINK . . . . . . .All routes FREE, including the Sealynx and the incredible Stena HSS to Eire

LE SHUTTLE . . . . .NO BIKES at the time of going to press, but the situation is under review

---

spare for clothes and so on. Put all the heaviest stuff in the small bag you are allowed to take as hand baggage and it's flying free.

Preparing the bike: The bike must be made into as flat a parcel as possible, so remove the pedals, turn the handlebars around and tape them to the crossbar, push the saddle down as far as it will go and let the tyres down so they don't explode at 30,000ft.

Protect the bike as well as you can. A custom made fibreglass case is safest, but will take you over the allowance into extra charges. A cycle bag will prevent scratches but on many occasions will not be stout enough.

I argue that if a bike looks like a bike it will be treated better. I use plumbers pipe lagging taped securely to protect the tubes. When you arrive at your destination, hide the lagging behind a billboard – it's almost certain to be there when you return.

Tell them it's coming: Warn the airline you would like to take the bike as your allowance just in case there are fifty others wanting to do the same.

Fingers crossed: The care of your bike at the far end will depend entirely on your destination. If it is a cycle friendly country like Italy you may have your bike brought off the plane first and presented to you with great civility; if it's Crete it will probably pop out on to the carousel with all the other luggage! Take sufficient tools to effect most repairs.

EXPEDITION BIKES

If you're in the wilds anywhere there are two things you must be sure of with your bike – it must be reliable and easy to fix if it breaks. This is doubly important in remote and unsophisticated parts of the world.

Go for a simple cold drawn steel frame (most steel mountain bikes are cold drawn, this just means none of the fancy heat-treated stuff). You can find basic welding equipment which will repair it almost anywhere in the world.

The newer the equipment the greater the reliability, but don't take a brand new bike on a big trip. Get your expedition bike a few weeks before you set off, ride it a lot, get it thoroughly bedded in and iron out any niggles.

Don't take worn out gear and hope that it will last. Sod's Law says it will collapse in the remotest place on earth.

Wheels take a hammering on expeditions, the poor bike turns into a pack mule and the spokes go ping! You never break a spoke at home, but the extra weight could prove fatal. Take two or three spares, they can also be used as splints for broken chainstays and panniers. A small epoxy resin kit can also fix a thousand things.

Expedition kit

In the remoter places you'll stick to the roads, they're horrendous enough usually, so you'll not be carrying the bike on your shoulder. That makes panniers the load carrying choice.

It is important to spread the load and maintain the balance of the bike. For this reason, although it's more expensive, use both front and rear panniers.

Pannier racks: Front pannier racks have a greater tendency to vibrate loose. This can be cured by the use of Nylok nuts – a type of locknut with a nylon insert which grips the thread of the bolt tightly – but check them regularly just the same. And take spares!

Aluminium alloy racks are strong, very light, but give little warning of breakage and the chances of getting them welded are extremely limited. Tubular steel racks are heavier, just as strong if not stronger, and any garage with a welding kit can fix them. They are often the choice of the serious expeditioner.

Panniers: There is a tremendous choice of panniers, and the destination will have a bearing on your requirements. Overall, they need to be durable,

Motorised back-up lessens the chance of a major breakdown.

with extra rubbing plates on the back; secure, preferably with some sort of quick release clip; and as waterproof as possible.

If you are going to Iceland or Norway you need them double waterproof – invest in the Karrimor Aquashield range!

A light or super reflective top is also a good idea, not only from a road safety point of view, but you can write on them, listing the contents, which saves a lot of scratching about if you are carrying four.

Water, water!

Water purification and transport are of paramount importance on any expedition, even in the UK. In hot countries the first thing on your mind will be your supply of pure water.

Camelbaks have gone a long way to solving the problem in temperate climates, but in hot countries several litres must be carried at times. Several large water bottles are one answer, custom building a special bottle cage to fit within the frame, or holding an even larger container on top of the pannier rack or racks is even more effective.

Purification

Effective water purification has always been difficult, but filtration systems have become very effective. If you have to take water from streams, a good filter is essential, even in developed countries, where pesticides find their way into the watercourses and animals foul the streams.

Ceramic filters are excellent, but expensive.

The General Ecology (Europe) Microlite system, on the other hand, fits on to standard bike bottles, and weighs only 240g. It removes herbicides, sediment, colour, cysts, pesticides, foul tastes, giardia, algae, organics, odours, asbestos and cryptosporidium!

It's definitely well worth taking on your holidays; filtering the water goes a long way towards defeating the dreaded Delhi Belly.

If your Bobbins 2000 hydro thust lever fails out here it's a long walk back. Stick with tried and tested bikes and bits.

CHAPTER 6

wheels
on the ground
competition

RACING FOR FUN, CROSS-COUNTRY

COMPETITION, YOUR FIRST

RACE, ORIENTEERING EVENTS

Justin Loretz is *MBUK*'s staff writer. Brought up on the mag from his early teens, he's a dreadful warning of what it can do to an impressionable young mind. Classy downhill and XC racer.

Derek's left you dreaming of the silent magnificence of the high hills. I'm here to bring you back down to earth into the colour, crowds and noise of mountain bike events, the race tapes flapping in the wind, the typical smells of local catering and portaloos and the group buzz that hovers over an event venue all weekend, a heady mixture of adrenalin, testosterone and raw fear.

There are competitions for all the skills in mountain biking. Wheels on the ground competition means the various types of cross-country racing, with a tip of the hat to the orienteering-type events, which are semi-

GOING
RACING

When someone says they race, be it pigeons or mountain bikes, it's usually assumed they're in with a good chance of coming out the winner, or are, at the very least, a contender for the top. The cool thing about mountain biking is that it is possible to 'go racing' regardless of your physical ability, the condition of your bike or your mental state.

competitive expedition riding. Jason McRoy deals with downhilling and its offshoots in Chapter 7.

Most events have some scope for more than one discipline, some, like the Karrimor Series (see below), cater for most of them all in one weekend.

If you've read cycling mags that aren't *MBUK*, you'll have got the impression that MTB events are all about cross-country racing and that racing is all about fitness, nutrition, pain and the will to win.

You'll probably be expecting all sorts of training charts and diet sheets here. Well, forget it.

They're not here for two very good reasons: the sort of general training plans you get in books and magazines are almost useless, and mountain bike races aren't about that anyway.

Except at the very top. The great majority of us haven't

Racing for an honest crust. Life's tough at the top, eh.

The thrills of competition are great but the racing life isn't for everyone.

Some days you wonder if it wouldn't have been a better idea staying in bed.

the physical ability to reach the very top, no matter how hard we train, and plenty of those who have aren't prepared to let competition take over their lives completely, which is pretty much what you have to do if you're going to podium big time.

The rest of us go racing for fun. The racing is basically the focus for a great big social get-together. The competitive instinct is strong, but it's not that crucial. If you're the kind of rider who has bike-throwing temper tantrums when you get beat, learn to hide it or you'll get laughed off the face of the earth.

Competitive or what?

Which does not mean the ordinary racer/eventer is not highly competitive. Almost all mountain bikers are. Take yourself. When you are out riding and see another bike on the trail either ahead of you or coming up from behind, do you put a spurt on and ride like a nutter to catch or pull away from the other rider?

If you do (and I'll bet that's almost all of you), you have the competitive spirit. If you respond to and enjoy this type of occasional trail challenge you will really get off on competition at some level.

But you can compete among friends anyway, so why bother going to an organised event?

The why of it

Every weekend thousands of ordinary mountain bikers trade their local trails for the stripy taped confines of the race course. Why? I do it because I like to go fast. In fact I like to go full out while there are trails where it's safe to do that. Most of the time you're restrained by the thought that just around that corner the Swiss Family Gormless is waiting to pop out from among the blackberry bushes. On a closed course you can really let rip!

Then there's the social side – every bit as important. Mountain bike events are as much a chance to catch up on the latest gossip and muck about with my mates as they are about riding. Pasta parties, the beer tent filled with all the booze and junk food you've spurned before the race, the chance to chill out, hang out and meet other bike nutters.

I can handle it

Careful, though, you can get hooked. For some people, once is enough; they come, take part, and for the most part enjoy the experience; but as

Ned Overend is pushing 40 and still kicking the butts of guys half his age.

soon as it's over they write 'been there, done that' in the box marked MTB events and go back to happily riding their bikes on the open trail.

But for those who compete regularly (more than five times a year), it becomes more than just a chance to test their techniques and cardiovascular system, it becomes a potent drug. The amounts of adrenalin and endorphins released into the body before and during the event supply a very real rush. Light headedness, butterflies and sweaty palms are all sure signs that your body is preparing itself for battle.

The feeling at the time is hard to describe but in the warm afterglow you experience for a few days after the end of a race, it all begins to make more sense. When the memory of that great pass you made on the tricky singletrack flashes across your mind in vivid technicolour your pulse quickens and you get that funny taste in your mouth that you only get when racing (and just before you puke). Your body reacts like an old war horse – it can get to the stage where just seeing some brilliant riding on video can trigger the reaction.

You're hooked

After a few weeks back riding the home trails the addicted racer gets the urge. Yep, the racing gland is swollen again and when this happens there is only one cure. The feeling and the flashbacks to previous races build until attendance becomes inevitable. So you go to another event, and the more you go the stronger the pull is to go again.

You are now officially addicted to mountain biking and in particular to races. Note I said races – not racing – there is a distinct difference.

It's at this point that you have to stay in control. If you relax for a second you can easily get sucked into the quest for RESULTS. As soon as the R word becomes the driving force for entering events you, by default, join the serious minority.

The serious minority

The minority are the 'racer' racers. These are the serious guys and gals for whom Sundays are very much a working day. They are motivated to spend all their waking hours each week thinking about what they are going to do for two hours on a Sunday.

If you decide you have what it takes to win then by all means commit to racing, but be warned, racing tunnel vision will set in! With very few exceptions all racers of this type can see is the finishing line, and

Overleaf – The ranks of riders who race for a laugh; they don't care who wins.

THE ANTI-RACE RACERS

The best example of 'Anti-Race Racers' is the Mint Sauce Race and Flowers Team. The rules of membership for this crack squad of highly under-trained and overfed individuals explain the whole anti-race thing:

■ Racing as you and I know it, is not permitted – however, riding with a bunch of friends with numbers on their bikes is.

■ While 'not-racing', courtesy should be shown to all fellow 'riding-fast non-competitors'. Hold gates open for people, even if open already. Stop to help anyone with a puncture and chat happily to spectators.

■ The only time that overtaking is allowed is when climbing hills. For this purpose it is recommended that you run a MicroDrive-style chainset with a normal (12-32) block; this will enable you to climb every hill in your big ring, thus demoralising everyone in time for the screaming descent.

■ Descents should be approached with caution and plenty of brakes. Wearing dark glasses will help you to ignore the gradient. Descend slowly, while chanting 'Don't look at the tree, don't look at the tree'. At the bottom of the slope, dismount, kiss the ground and thank the Lord, Supreme Being or tree spirits (pick one) for your safe deliverance.

■ After not-racing, make straight for the tea-tent (after changing into new, clean, white team strip) and consume as much food and drink as possible. Then retire gracefully to the team van for the drive home, accompanied by suitably mellow tunes while little pink flowers stream out of the exhaust... or something.

ARE YOU A PHOBIC?

The Anti-Race Racers love races but, for many mountain bikers, taking part in a large organised event represents everything they started the sport to avoid: lots of noise, crowds, corporate images and money. Some can't stand the thought of competition in any form.

If these are the things you started mountain biking to get away from then you're in the category of riders who won't enjoy mountain bike races. The orienteering events might suit you, though.

---

gradually everything else in their lives begins to revolve around racing. Even relationships with families and partners have to be reshaped if they are to survive.

Most full time amateur racers still manage to have a little fun here and there, but the serious side of their nature is never far away. Given the choice between styling a cool jump for the crowd and passing another rider, the results racer will nearly always go for the place (the opposite can be said of fun and sports class riders). In extreme cases the ability to retain a rounded outlook on life disappears, they do become humourless, characterless shadows who train hard, race and go home to train harder still without so much as telling one nob gag all weekend.

It's a dedication you admire in a professional, but in an amateur it's all a bit sad.

The majority (you and me)

The dedication, pain and upheaval required to get

Just grin and bear it. Sod's Law says that sooner or later you'll end up wearing the trail.

on to the podium is all fine and dandy if you are a sponsored rider with the raw talent and genes (genetic not denim) to win. But the number of people capable of pushing themselves at maximum output for two hours and whose max is higher than anyone else in the field is small. Out of the hundreds of people who take part at the event there is only a slack handful with a chance of winning.

Time for a reality check. The chances are, without wanting to sound defeatist, that you're not one of them. With this in mind, you must strike a fine balance between the time and effort you devote to your mountain biking and the goals you can realistically hope to achieve.

Once you decide you're not podium material then the whole thing changes. While the racing racers watch their diet like religious fanatics and train

'Deadly Nedly' Overend is such a great example of 'a cool dude who races', here's another picture.

like obsessives (on road bikes at night in the rain is obsessive), people racing just for the blast eat chips and drink beer. This is all OK. One of the best aspects of mountain bike racing at the lower levels is that you can do pretty much what you like in between times and still enjoy it.

You can still do well too, although there are some, like the anti-race racers (see page 86), who enjoy their racing but would rather die than do well.

I'M A RACER!

Right you've made the decision to devote what free time you have to being a mountain bike racer. You can now officially tell all and sundry that you are a racer. Take my advice – don't!

"Hi!, I'm a mountain bike racer" is one of the worst chat up lines ever. The person you are trying to impress usually says:

"Wow! You race motorbikes!" Imagining all sorts of leather clad action.

"No, no MOUNTAIN BIKES," you reply.

"Oh you're one of those people I see on the towpath wearing those tight, black shorts!"

Aaaarrrggg!!!!

Training

As a 'mountain bike racer' you will want to do all the things pro bike racers do when they are not competing. Like training.

As I said right at the beginning, general training plans aren't a heap of use, ideally a plan needs to be tailored to your needs by a qualified coach who understands your physical talents and what you're aiming to achieve. What follows is just to give you a general idea of the kind of thing you're letting yourself in for.

First the basic question – what is training?

It's a systematic way of stressing your body and allowing it to adapt to

Mountain bikers on road bikes? Miles on the road count for fitness off them.

Trials riding is big fun. Practise your skills wherever you can sit on your bike.

the stress so it can handle it in the future. To do that, the body needs recovery time. So typically you increase the stress gradually for, say, three weeks and then have a less intense recovery week before stressing it again. Without recovery time you won't improve, you'll just slog yourself into the ground.

Second, a more specific question – what sort of training does mountain bike racing require?

Three sorts:

■ Endurance fitness, which means getting in the miles regularly and progressively over a long period of time, like two years.

■ Power training, which means hill work, in practice, both short and sharp and long drags.

■ Speed training, which means high intensity sprint work and intervals. The endurance part you can start now, it means getting out on your bike more, increasing the time spent and the intensity with proper recovery time. For the rest, seek out a coach at your local cycling club or sports centre and take more specific advice. Here's the sort of advice you might get if you wanted to improve at sports class in a year's time:

October – December: 8 hours a week, spread over three or four rides all at moderate pace. Remember the recovery weeks.

January: 8-10 hours (1-2 hours hard, 6-8 hours moderate).

February – March: 2 hours hard, mixing up 1 hour steady rate with one hour of sprints or short (15 seconds) steep climbs; 4 hours moderate, 1-2 hours easy.

March – April: 2 hours hard, mixing up 1 hour steady rate with 30 minutes very fast and three bursts of 10 minutes flat out; 2 hours easy; 2 hours moderate.

Race season: 1-2 hours easy the day after the race, 4-6 hours during the week.

You can increase the intensity to peak for big events, but this is getting into pro territory and requires very personalised training.

■ Don't panic! You don't have to do all this! If you're happy to be moderately competitive in the sports class or lower, ride your bike plenty, have fun and do a bit of cross training and you'll be fit enough to enjoy the races.

Cross training

Cross training is the trendy term for doing sports other than the one you are training for, as training. This means combining light amounts of running, swimming, weights, circuits, rollerblading, aerobics, even racquet sports into your training regime.

Cross training has two main advantages. One is that you gain a wide base of fitness by exercising muscle groups that mountain biking doesn't stress. The other, just as important, is that taking part in other activities keeps you from getting stale and bored with bikes.

It's fun and easy to arrange. Your local sports centre has trained instructors who will be able to point you in the direction of circuit training classes, weight rooms, swimming lanes evenings and, even better, other sports people of the same level as you – a group of runners, say.

Get as much free help from the trained instructors as you can and make contact with groups of like minded people who are all trying to train for their own sports. Training alone is a sure fire way to get demoralised, get lazy or fall into bad habits. There is nothing like having someone there to make you swim the extra length, do the extra rep, or run the extra mile. Any athlete will tell you the extra motivation of working out with others is all important.

The diet thing

Many riders embark on a 'full on' winter training regime, intent on becoming stronger, faster riders who won't have sand metaphorically kicked in their faces next season. That's fine unless, the moment they get home after doing another load of good work in the gym, they blow it with a double portion of egg'n'chips and a (non Diet) Coke, followed by half a packet of biscuits or, God forbid, they pop the top of a tube of Pringles!

With that sort of fuel going into the engine it's game over before you've even got to the start line.

No need to get faddy about diet. You need plenty of carbohydrates from pasta, jacket spuds, rice, bread, that sort of thing, and the sort of minerals and vitamins that fresh fruit and veg, nuts and fish provide.

Cutting down on the sugary, fatty foods won't be hard. Once you start all that exercise and begin to speed up your metabolism you will feel like eating different foods anyway. After a good sweaty session, which would you rather neck, a bag of crisps, a couple of choc bars and a milkshake, or a tasty pasta salad dish with some nice wholemeal rolls, a couple of pieces of fruit and some ice cold mineral water?

Give me the second option every time.

The proof of the pudding is in the winning (preferably with custard for Tim Gould). For the pros, nothing short of first place will do.

The bike

I've got an Ultra Bog Standard Thingummy, can I race it? That's the number 1 race-related query we get at *MBUK*. The answer is almost always, yes – provided they're set up properly (see Chapter 2), most mountain bikes are raceable.

Some are more raceable than others. You'll find a bike under £250 very hard work, compared with a bike costing just £100 more.

You can spend thousands on a bike, of course, but there are disadvantages to having a top bike – like what are you going to blame for coming 86th?

Performance really is down to the rider, not the bike, but it's no good having a brilliantly prepared body and a total wreck of a bike. A couple of weeks before you are due to race take your bike to your local bike shop for a once over and a service (if it needs it). If you already take pretty good care of your bike you should only have to follow these checks:

Ten pre-race checks

As with aircraft, your bike needs regular pre-flight checks.

✿ Check all nuts and bolts for tightness. They should be tight but they should not be screamingly tight. In most cases the bolts are steel and the

The king of all mountain bike racers is US rider John Tomac. Just watch his style and learn all you can from it.

parts they screw into are alloy which makes it easier than you think to strip the thread on expensive Shimano thumbshifters (don't I know it).

⚙ Spin your wheels to check they are no more than 2-3mm out of true (side to side wobble) and your spokes are intact and evenly tensioned.

⚙ Check your brakes. Look at the pads to check for wear, and replace if necessary. Cables should run freely; if they don't, change them. Give the levers a spot of lube.

⚙ Check your gears. If they are stiff, replace the cables and give the levers some lube. If the outer cables (brake or gear) have kinks or small splits in them, chuck them out and fit fresh ones.

⚙ Make sure that the chain runs freely and has no stiff links. Massage some lube well into the links with a cloth to get it right inside the chain.

⚙ Examine the frame for cracks, terminal rust and fruitbats. The most common areas to find a potential failure are on the top and down tubes just behind the head tube and in Surrey. A suspect frame should not be raced.

⚙ Check your tyres for wear. A bald tyre is of little use in the mud.

⚙ Check your bar and stem for tightness. A slipping seatpost or spinning bar is a nightmare as you begin lap two.

⚙ Check that your cranks are on tight and spin your pedals to check they are fine. If you are not used to riding with toe straps or clipless pedals then the day before the race is not the time to fit them.

⚙ Fit a water bottle cage (or two) and get used to using it on the move.

Which event?

The standard short course, multi-lap cross-country race is by far and away the most common and the type most likely to please budding boy racers. There are two types to choose from: the two National Series, the Karrimor and BMB (well organised, catering for all levels, but awkward to

Raleigh pro Barrie Clarke enjoys another hard day at the office.

Overleaf – To get to the top races you have to train hard.

CROSS-COUNTRY CONTACTS

ENGLAND

Governing body: British Mountain Biking, The National Cycling Centre, 1 Stuart Street, Manchester M11 4DQ
☎ 0161 223 2244
National series entries. Send an SAE to:
The Karrimor Series: Karrimor International Ltd, Petre Road, Clayton-le-Moors, Accrington BB5 5JZ
The National Points Series: BMB Entries, Postwood, Kentisbeare, Cullompton, Devon EX15 2BS

WALES

The Welsh Cycling Union, Gunnarside, 4 Orme View Drive, Prestatyn, Clwyd LL19 9PF

SCOTLAND

Scottish Cycling Union, The Velodrome, Meadowbank Stadium, London Road, Edinburgh EH7 6AD

CONTACTS

ORIENTEERING CONTACTS

Polaris: Challenge Events, 87 Hollins Spring Avenue, Dronfield nr Sheffield, Derbyshire S18 6RP
Trailquest: Trail Cyclists Association, Raycomb Lane, Ledbury, Hertfordshire HR8 1JH

---

get to) and local races (on the whole, less well organised, but convenient).

Less common are point to point races in which you don't ride the same ground twice. These are typically longer than multi lap races and consequently tend to draw more experienced riders to the event.

MBUK is particularly useful for easy to follow information on races and events at local, regional, national and international levels. Also keep a look out in your local bike shops and in your local paper for details of races near you.

Orienteering events

For a lot of riders, careering round and round a short course is simply not mountain biking. They prefer events which are as close to real expedition riding as possible, with the added spice of competition (if you want to) and the social buzz of a big occasion.

Two events have become incredibly popular recently:

Polaris: A multi day mountain bike orienteering event for teams of two or more riders. The teams have directions to a number of checkpoints (the more difficult to reach, the more points they're worth) dotted about the countryside. Each team of riders can visit the checkpoints in any order that they like. At the end of the event the points are totted up and – you guessed it – the team with the most points wins.

Competitors camp overnight and are totally self-sufficient during the event (if you can't ride with it on your bike, you can't use it).

Polaris is well worth trying, but it's a real test of endurance and self-sufficiency, run in autumn and early spring in the hope of some challenging weather.

True Polaris lovers are only really happy if they wake up to find their balaclavas frozen to their tents (right Derek?).

Trailquest: These are single day orienteering events which can be tough, but cater for a much wider range of abilities than Polaris. They are becoming very popular both as a competitive or non-competitive activity and are run relatively frequently. There is a Trailquest event every month of the year except December.

RACING CROSS-COUNTRY

The multi-lap, short course cross-country race is your most likely entry to competition – there are lots of them (it is now possible to race a variety of events every weekend of the year) and they're the least likely to cause you any real problems.

In fact you're going to enjoy them a lot. Especially if you go mob handed. If you are new to racing, blackmail a few of your mates into having a go with you. The more you can get to go, the less stressful the whole thing becomes.

What class?

Pick the right class. Too easy and you won't be challenged, too hard and you'll get disillusioned. Organisers call their classes by different names, but there's almost always a 'fun class' (a short race for the less than dedicated) and a 'novice class' (a longer, more serious race, for newbies).

If you're reading this, these are probably your aim. Above that is the sports class, where you'll find some excellent riders, then the experts and at the top, the pro/elite class where the gods hang out. There are also classes for sprogs and juniors (older sprogs) and for veterans and masters (older veterans), all of them open to men and women.

Entering a race

Once you have decided on an event, you call or send an SAE to the organisers for an entry form. Remember that the earlier you can get your entry in the better your chances of getting a place.

Fill out your entry form marking which class you would like to race in and make a note of exactly what it is you are getting for your money. Some organisers put on a pasta party the night before the race and often give all finishers a T-shirt with something like 'I was a finisher of the Bob Nobody Classic MTB race' emblazoned across the chest. No marks for style but a nice memento all the same.

All that is left for you to do is wait for the big day. Almost.

The night before

Check, double check, triple check, pack, un-pack (just to check) and re-pack again. 'Why?' you may ask. Well, nothing ruins a weekend's mountain bike racing more than turning up with only one shoe.

At one time or another this sort of disaster has befallen every mountain biker. The most extreme example I have seen is a man turning up to a race minus his bike. He'd asked his teenage son to take his bike from the garage and put it in the boot the night before and, well... that's teenagers for you.

Nerves

I know mountain bikers who race at a very high level and still get in all

Whoops! Still, it's entertaining for the crowds, and there's always next year.

RACE KIT

The list of things to pack will vary from person to person but after you have been to a few races you will begin to get a better idea of what you feel comfortable travelling with (or should that be without?).
Have you packed the following?

- ⚙ Bike
- ⚙ Helmet, gloves and glasses
- ⚙ Cycling shoes and socks
- ⚙ Riding kit (two lots if the weather's bad)
- ⚙ Post race clothing
- ⚙ Wash kit and towel
- ⚙ Toolkit including spares and pump
- ⚙ Money
- ⚙ Food

---

kinds of trouble with nerves before events.

If you find that you just cannot sleep for worrying about the big day ahead, get up and go and polish your bike: frame, wheels, the lot. This may not send you to sleep but even if it doesn't, you can arrive bleary eyed at the race site happy in the knowledge that you have the best valeted bike there!

A good domestic season could see you on one of the international teams.

Seriously, there is no point in worrying about a mountain bike race, everyone is there to have fun and is not, I repeat not, going to stand there and laugh at you as you pootle by.

Race day

On the morning of the race a good breakfast – cereal, toast, coffee and some juice – will help settle pre-race jitters.

Don't consume large amounts of food less than two hours before the start of your race – not only are you likely to puke it all over the guy in front but it won't have had time to be digested and isn't any real good to you. If you must have something in the final run up to the start, nibble a PowerBar, but if you eat these high performance energy bars be sure to take on plenty of water so the vital vitamins and minerals are absorbed into your stomach walls faster.

Take plenty of liquid on board, slowly. Sipping water or a sports fluid replacement drink every few minutes on the morning of the event will stop you dehydrating and cramping, without making you feel bloated.

Getting there

You have enough things to think about without adding the stress of having to drive hundreds of miles. Bribe a friend to drive you. Not only does this take a load off your mind but in the event of you hugging a tree they will be able to drive you to hospital or, in an extreme case, a tree surgeon.

Leave with plenty of time allowed for fuel, wee and munchy stops and getting lost along the way.

You're there!

When you arrive on site take five minutes to get your bearings – work out where your car is parked in relation to the toilets, race headquarters, the start/finish line and the food.

Now go to the signing on tent where they should have your race numbers ready for you. Make sure you have the correct number of pins and zip ties to secure them to your shirt and bike and do it! Sounds daft, but many racers forget until the last minute when they are in a mad rush to get to the start line.

Next, check out the course. You can't go fast unless you know what you are riding over. It also helps you decide where you want your moral support. If your driver/helper is going to hand you a water bottle during the race make sure they give it to you on a slow part of the track – a wide, smooth, gentle incline is preferable. When you are happy you know what the course looks like, go back to the paddock area and CHILL OUT.

Warm up

With about 45 minutes to go to your start time get changed and go for a warm-up ride. A warm-up ride is essential to get the blood flowing and your heart pumping so when the gun goes for the start you're ready for instant action.

The next stop is the start.

The start (and beyond)

Fun class riders, relax! When the starter's flag drops, all you have to do is pedal your bike and enjoy yourselves. If you're in a more serious class, the start is mega important.

When the race starts there is usually a manic rush to the bottleneck where the first singletrack begins. The first twenty or so riders get through, the rest are left in a jostling mass. Get stuck here and you can

Top riders like Missy Giove know the value of warming up before the start of a race.

expect to lose about 45 seconds to a minute before getting properly going. That time is really hard to make up so, if you can be in that first twenty or thereabouts, you have less work to do. Get as close to the front of the grid as you can and really hammer those first five minutes. Ignore the symptoms of 'start' panic.

It may not feel like panic, but the start of a race will do strange things to you. It is usual to feel as though you are riding through a field of treacle on a unicycle. Breathing is hard, you may feel sick, but don't worry because everyone else feels this way. After the initial panic of the first five minutes you will begin to settle down and actually enjoy the sensation.

Don't pull out!

During the race, use your natural skills to your advantage, if you know you are very good at climbing or descending then try to make the time spent doing them count double.

The only other thing to be wary of is the desire to pull out. Whatever you do, don't! When you get that feeling, drop right down to your lowest gear and twiddle for five minutes. Get your breath back, have a sip of water and a nibble of PowerBar, and when you feel you can, step back on the gas.

The finish line will arrive, hopefully, sooner rather than later. Once you have crossed it, the feeling of achievement is huge.

No matter how much your legs hurt and your lungs burned while you were riding, five minutes after you have finished you will feel great!

flying

D O W N H I L L   R A C I N G ,   E Q U I P M E N T ,

S T A R T I N G   O U T ,   D O W N H I L L   T E C H N I Q U E ,

T H E   I N T E R N A T I O N A L   S C E N E

Jason McRoy is Britain's top downhiller. A long time contributor and Team MBUK rider, he is now an international star with Team Specialized. Unlike most great riders Jase can explain exactly how he does it.
The MTB wheel has turned full circle. It all started with a few crazy Yanks flying their bikes down mountains. But then, I guess, cross-country suited the blazer-wearing cycling establishment better and downhill became the juvenile delinquent of the scene.

It's taken over five years for downhilling to regain its cred, but now it's top of the heap in image terms. That's because it's practically made for TV, with its maximum visual impact, its fast, immediate action, its outlandish kit and even more outlandish personalities.

Downhill is cool, and the good news is you can jump on a bike and go and do it yourself.

Attitude
The rise of downhilling reflects the return of the carefree rebel attitude to mountain biking, after years of grim, hard-grinding cross-country. The two disciplines are worlds apart.

There are some cross-country riders who can compete at a high level in downhill, just as there are some vicars who drink, swear and go around with fast women, but when it comes down to it the events and the people who do them couldn't be more different.

It's all to do with attitude, and a healthy dose of adrenalin. A lung-bursting grind up an impossible gradient might be a satisfying challenge to a cross-country joe, but to a downhiller, it's a waste of time and effort. It's far better to be storming down an impossible gradient, riding to the limits of your abilities.

True downhilling is a state of MTB nirvana, where rider and bike are pushed to the limit, where you know you are only barely in control, where the adrenalin rush has to be counteracted by the knowledge that what you are doing is incredibly dangerous.

And you don't have three hours to repair mechanicals and get back time lost through mistakes. A downhill race rarely lasts more than five minutes. In these five minutes you have to ride your lines to perfection, be completely

focused and pray that the bike/tyres/gears will hold up. Less than 100 per cent concentration and you're a loser.

It's a different state of mind. Frenetic is the word. Emotionally frenetic, a frenetic lifestyle and a love of speed; mix these elements, put them on a bike and you've got a downhiller.

The look

Cross-country and downhill riders look different, both on and off the bike. Downhillers are going for low air-drag bodysuits over their armour while cross-country riders are content to chug around in the standard Lycra top and shorts. Casual wear for a downhiller is likely to be mega-trendy and outrageous, while most cross-country riders will settle for a sweatshirt or T-shirt and a pair of jeans or shorts (let's face it, they're boring!).

Getting started

Before you even think of downhilling seriously, remember this: cross-country can be dangerous, downhilling is always extremely dangerous.

Speaking for myself, despite the pain and disappointment I've suffered in the sport (and there's been plenty), there's nothing in the world I'd rather do than be out there competing on my bike in the downhill.

But beware! One good result and you'll end up chasing victory like a greyhound after a rabbit. It'll be in your blood, you'll want to race properly, get fit, get a great bike and go looking for a sponsor...

So have you got what it takes? Ask yourself these questions:

■ Are you a good bike handler at high speed?
■ Can you handle a bike on slow, technical terrain?
■ Can you sprint well?
■ Can you focus on the job in hand?
■ Can you exclude pain from your mind?
■ Can you handle constant pressure from the public, your sponsor and yourself?
■ Can you read terrain? Can you plan good lines?
■ Do you know your own limits?
■ Do you know when to take risks?
■ And when not to?
■ Are you willing to take those risks?

If you want to be a good (and safe) downhiller, the only answer to all these questions is... yes.

So you really want to race

OK, let's get started. The least traumatic place to start your downhill career is a properly organised event in Britain.

By properly organised, I mean a Karrimor Series event, sanctioned by the North of England Mountain Bike Association (NEMBA), or one

Greg Herbold has been downhilling for years and knows how to look cool.

Riders like Mike King, Toby Henderson and Jake Watson have come from BMX to the downhill discipline and added their own distinctive style.

sanctioned by British Mountain Bike (BMB). Both organisations have been around long enough to know what they are supposed to be doing and they choose their organisers with care. Day licences can usually be bought if you are not quite sure how far you want to take your racing.

I don't want to put you off, but the other big plus is that both NEMBA and the BMB use experienced organisers who know just where to site their medical teams. At this stage in your career that's more important than the prizes on offer!

Forget the glamour

The UK is not a particularly mountainous place and, with a few notable exceptions, downhill venues tend to be technical rather than spectacularly fast. This makes it an excellent place to begin downhilling. In Europe and the United States they race down mountains.

The upside of mountains is that they have ski-lifts to the top. On British hills you have to ride to the start and by the time you've put in half a dozen practice runs, you feel as if you have been taking part in a cross-country event. Bear this in mind when setting up your gearing: a fifty-tooth chainring and a DCD look the business, but riding up the hill gets difficult.

THE DOWNHILL BIKE

Technically, the differences between cross-country and downhill hardware are enormous. A top flight downhill bike is closer to a motorised trail bike than it is to a standard mountain bike.

Front and rear suspension units are standard on most competitive machines with infinitely variable riding set-ups available. Weight is not as critical a factor in downhill as it is in cross-country, the most crucial element in the downhill bike's make-up being its strength and reliability.

Tyres and tubes are generally more robust and heavier for the downhill scene but despite the advent of puncture-proof tubes, puncturing is still the commonest reason for a DNF.

The right bike

Buying a full-blown downhill machine won't get you on the podium above Tomac. Buying the right bike will enhance your skills, nothing else. When you're taking up downhilling, you've three options:

■ Adapt a standard, entry-level racing MTB, making small and relatively cheap alterations.
■ Adapt a mid-range bike with more expensive and dramatic alterations.
■ Raid Granny's biscuit tin and buy yourself a top dog downhill bike.

The budget option: Budget doesn't mean cheap. You must have a strong, reputable bike to take the strain, which means something around £400-£500.

Change the handlebars – the narrower the bar, the less control you have over your bike. Don't go over the top, you can go too wide, especially if you have narrow shoulders – 22-25in should do most people. Removing your bar ends also gives you extra width.

Replace the brake system. There are many good brakes on the market at different price points, Graftons and Maguras are the best (and most expensive), or try XT or XTR. Replacement blocks are expensive but give good stopping power if you set them up right.

Fit a DCD – It's an invaluable gadget from Sensible Products that keeps your chain on over rough track at maximum flog. Well worth the £19.99 – a dropped chain can cost you more time than a crash.

Check out the tyres – if you don't already have them, change to fatties for maximum comfort and traction.

Mid-priced option: A mid-priced bike at £700-£800 will have excellent components. Modify it as you would the budget bike, and fit suspension forks. Your choice will depend on your style, your budget (you'll spend between £200 and £600), and your prejudices.

With these mods, your bike's starting to look and feel the part.

Top Dog option: Nothing better than the best, but you really need some experience before you will know what is best for you. The full suspension bike will part you from £1,500 for an entry level machine to £4,500 for one of the top of the range bikes. Every manufacturer claims to have the best bike, but they all have their own good and bad points. Read the reports and try before you buy. Remember, the bike is only as good as its pilot...

Setting up your bike

On some courses you barely need to pedal, on others you're pedalling all the time – some British downhills actually go up in places! The course determines how you set up your bike.

Saddle height: On a course with relatively easy technical sections, your saddle will be near your regular cross-country height; on a difficult course with limited pedalling, it should be much lower – to take advantage of the lowered centre of gravity in high speed cornering and to make it easier to move around on the bike when things get tricky. (See Chapter 8).

Tyre pressure: If you don't have suspension, lower pressures give you more traction, smooth out the ride but raise the risk of a pinch puncture. With suspension it's nothing like so important. I generally run a high tyre pressure with a big tyre to lessen the chances of puncturing. You sacrifice traction, but with only one run to prove yourself, I'd rather slide around a little than have to walk to the finish...

Gearing: Don't take any notice of what everyone else is choosing. Find a gear you feel comfortable with and discount the theory that the person who pushes the biggest gear can travel the fastest. In the '93 Vail Grundig I used a 50T (fifty-tooth) chainring and clocked the fastest speed of the

Jason McRoy corners at speed on the Downhill at Vail.

Downhill body armour and a full face helmet lessen the chances of injury.

THE GREAT RACE – THE HEAD TO HEAD ELIMINATOR

The original, made-for-TV, Reebok Eliminator was devised in the USA. Bill Cockroft of the Mammoth Mountain Ski Resort (who also brought dual slalom to the masses), thought that the Kamikaze was becoming tame, so he created an event in 1992 that brought together the world's top downhillers in a head-to-head race down the Kamikaze course.

Each rider gets two runs and the competitor with the fastest combined times goes into the next round. If you go through you have to head back to the start the moment you finish your run. Any mechanical problems have to be sorted on top of the mountain.

With thirty two competitors in the men's race, the two finalists have raced 35 miles down Mammoth Mountain.

I reached the finals in 1993, racing against Myles Rockwell. After our two runs down the course, seven miles in all, the total combined time difference in Myles's favour was seventeen hundredths of a second! It's that close.

As if downhilling against the clock wasn't hard enough, Dual Eliminator competitors duel it out elbow to elbow.

day. Tomac was using something close to 60T; Dave Cullinan had a 46T on his bike, yet was only 1mph slower than me. As a guide, if you can't spin a gear out, you need a smaller gear. If you spin a gear out on 75 per cent of the course, you need a bigger gear. Shift the emphasis from gear selection to braking and cornering more efficiently. There is not a downhill in this country where you need a bigger chainring than 48T to do well.

Suspension: British courses are fairly standard in terms of technical difficulty. If you have suspension, you need as much shock travel as possible without your suspension bottoming out. Rear suspension should also be set to its maximum performance, having the most travel without bottoming out or making the bike bob too much when you're pedalling hard. It's trial and error, but as your experience grows, you should be able to set up a bike close to your ideal simply through riding the course a couple of times.

The bits that break

Downhill puts lots of strain on equipment, and failure at 50mph is catastrophic. Get the best kit and check it regularly.

■ Before every run check out the condition of your frame, especially around welded areas. If there any signs of cracking, then the frame should be replaced; this is ultimately cheaper and infinitely preferable to having

the broken frame surgically removed from your body.

You can abuse a good steel frame much more than you can an aluminium one, and if your budget is limited, steel is a better buy.

■ Bars and stems are a danger point. Don't buy light kit for downhilling. Check them and change them often.

■ Don't skimp on the wheels. For downhill it is better to spend extra money on having your wheels professionally built. They will last longer and stay truer longer and, personally speaking, having folded several mass-market wheels, using good strong wheels is one thing less to worry about when racing.

Spares

Breaking bits and pieces is annoying, time-consuming and expensive but it's also an integral part of the sport, so remember to pack a basic spares kit when you go off to race.

Include spare tyres and tubes, brake blocks, chainrings (46T-50T are sufficient for racing in Great Britain), elastomers for that type of fork, a

Myles Rockwell set new records at the 1995 Kamikaze and Reebok Eliminator.

spare chain and any spares for all those fancy imported widgets you've put on your bike.

Take a good track pump, a good, basic toolkit and a fork pump (if you're running air/oil forks).

Protective clothing

As spares for your body are pretty hard to carry around, you will have to decide on some form of protective wear.

■ A helmet is compulsory, but even the best helmet in the world won't do its job properly if it doesn't fit. Make sure yours does. I recommend a full-face helmet; a face-down endo in the gravel at 50mph will do nothing for your social life.

■ Gloves are also becoming compulsory in many races abroad.

■ Full body armour. Not compulsory and I don't think it should be. To start with, body armour always made me think about crashing which sapped my confidence, but I'm slowly coming round to accepting it as a benefit, not a hindrance.

Body armour doesn't make you invincible. It will save you from cuts and bruises in some crash situations, but broken bones are as common in people with body armour as without.

■ Knee and shin pads are a good idea.

■ Eye protection is essential – the correct eye protection. Remember that even on a sunny day it can be dark at some point on the downhill course, so if you're wearing the popular shade-type eye protection, make sure it has interchangeable clear or amber lenses and they're in your kit bag.

■ A brain. The best rider protection is the brain; good downhillers don't take their brains out to ride as is commonly suggested, they use them to ride within their limits.

Race tips

So you've found your event, paid your entry fee, picked up a day licence and you are ready to go. How do you handle it?

You should aim to have at least half a dozen practice runs before you race.

Walk the course – you see far more at a slower pace.

When it comes to race time, curb the adrenalin flow that courses through your body at the start. Anyone can go downhill fast, for a few hundred metres anyway, the trick is to ride within your limits so that you finish the course in one piece.

After you have one race under your belt, then you can set about raising your limits. This is done by sheer application, practice and experience. It is all down to you. After you have passed this baptism of fire and your UK results are consistently good, you can dabble in the international scene. The best place to do that is the Grundig Downhill Series.

At speeds in excess of 60mph, full face helmets are essential.

The new GT DH downhill bike features 5.5in of suspension movement.

THE INTERNATIONAL SCENE

If British downhills put butterflies in your innards, then the idea of competing in one of the Grundig World Cups will frighten the life out of you. Yes, there's the glamour that everyone talks about all around you, but you don't really notice any of that because you are so focused on what you have to do.

The 'friendliness' of the multinational competitors is legendary, but when you're nervous and tense, they could be swearing at you in their native tongues for all you know.

Some of the courses have to be seen to be believed, too. Some are so seemingly unridable that you wish you had brought your rock climbing harness with you!

However, once you have ridden what looked like an unridable track, you pass through another sphere of personal development.

When you get used to it you find the competitors are friendly and, in fact, tinged with the same form of madness which afflicts you – speedomania.

There are some pretty amazing places that you visit when you're on the international circuit (would you believe that there could be a mountain bike downhill race overlooking Monte Carlo?).

The courses themselves, both in Europe and America, are superb; the timing equipment is, on the whole, accurate, and start times religiously adhered to. This is a professional scene all right, and as such, is one that you're unlikely to experience until you've shown your worth in the home series, I fear.

From 1995, because of the high level of competition abroad and the extreme nature of the courses, it is proposed that only riders who have been nominated by their respective Federations will be able to compete in the World Cup.

YOU WANT TO BE A STAR?

If you think you've got what it takes to make it in the downhill big-time, go for it! To get recognition you have to ride in Europe, but to get the big team sponsorship you have to impress the Yanks, in the USA.

In 1992 I entered every European round of the Grundig Downhill Cup. It cost an absolute fortune, but I was working as well as being sponsored by *MBUK* and could afford it. I made 11th spot overall, and sat back and waited for the big rider deal. It never came.

In 1993 I knew I had to hit America. I decided to go for broke. My dad and I both took redundancy from BT and hit the Grundig circus with a vengeance. We did Cap d'Ail, Lillehammer and Kaprun in Europe and the entire US tour of Vail, Mammoth and New York.

What with air fares, accommodation and car hire, not to mention living expenses, we reached Mammoth skint, with our Visa cards in a very sorry state.

Before we left for the States, I sent my entry in for the Eliminator, by fax. The organisers were intrigued when they got my entry as they knew as little about me as I did about the race. After some telephonic persuasion on the part of my mother, they let me enter and I got my official invite at Vail after being fastest through the downhill speed trap (52mph – I've still got the Tag watch I won).

The rest, as they say, is history. I was second in the Eliminator by seventeen hundredths of a second to Myles Rockwell and followed up with my first British Championship. But it was my performance in the States that counted. Shortly after Christmas of that year I got a telephone call which started "I don't know if you remember me, but my name is Ned Overend and we met at Mammoth. Specialized USA would like to talk to you about joining their team...."

JASON McROY

New bike please. Downhilling can be dangerous for you and your bike.

GETTING THERE

Fitness

Contrary to popular belief, downhill racers are very, very fit. The fitness required to downhill is totally different to the fitness needed to succeed at cross-country. Downhill racing requires a lot of power used in full-out sprinting bursts; the same types of muscles which power Linford Christie to his sprint wins in 100 metre races are to be found on today's top downhill riders.

Piling on the miles works best for my overall fitness, combined with gymwork for upper body strength and a healthy mix of BMX racing, motocrossing and rollerblading to keep me sharp.

Abilities and skills

Fitness, a focused mental attitude and razor-sharp reactions are what you need. Quick reactions let you make adjustments to your line, your balance and riding position and gain extra milliseconds; if you have a blow-out or a

Hang it out. Sticking your inside leg out mid corner helps stabilise the bike.

bike-stopping mechanical at speed, your reactions had better be good!

Bike-handling skills must be honed to the nth degree, because when you are travelling fast, the slightest shift of body weight or the tiniest over-correction on steering can put you on the road to disaster. Messing around on BMX tracks is excellent for building bike handling ability and can teach you a thing or two about how your bike handles in different situations.

You must enjoy jumping your bike. It causes grief to many riders, yet with a little practice, jumping is one of your best allies. Everyone jumps at some time in a downhill. So go with the flow, don't fight the natural forces. Jumping is faster, more stylish and much more exciting than clinging to the ground.

You must be smooth. Your ultimate racing aim is smoothness at high speed. It's not easy. It is natural for the body to tense up after a hairy moment, but that leads to a very rough and sketchy ride. The pro way is to stay relaxed, even after you've made a mistake. And being dialled into the course stops you from panicking and taking the wrong line.

Smoothness takes work. It needs a special kind of focus, the kind that seems almost preternatural. In race mode, instead of thinking about the log in front of you, you should be focusing on the next switchback; clearing the log should be instinctive.

This only comes from constant practice. Don't just rush out on to your favourite ride and attack it as hard as you can – build your speed up slowly to increase your handling abilities gradually and give you a feeling for how your bike behaves at varying speeds.

It's important to be able to read a course beforehand, to suss out good and bad lines. Smooth is fast. Dramatic, on the edge riding only looks good. If your bike's drifting sideways, you're scrubbing off speed.

Faster, faster

Once you can downhill fast, you want to go faster, which is where judicious use of airtime comes in. One of the quickest ways over a hump is to speed-jump it, a time saving technique which could be more appropriately named the anti-jump. You maintain as much ground contact as possible on medium to large sized humps on the track (see chapter 8).

More foot out technique, from World Junior Downhill Champ Nicolas Vouilloz.

Go mental

The most common mental technique is visualisation, in which you imagine you're performing certain tasks – you imagine you're riding as smoothly and as quickly as possible, you run through every inch of the course in your head and visualise yourself having a perfect run, winning easily...

Masters of visualisation fool their subconscious into believing it; with that belief, your subconscious can make your body perform just as the visualisation showed.

THE DUAL SLALOM

Visually exciting, instant, spectator friendly and so easy to stage, dual slalom is growing in popularity with both crowds and downhillers. In true gladiatorial style, two competitors streak down a course slaloming, ski-style, between strategically placed poles before sprinting to the finish line. A complete run takes less than a minute and the spectators love it.

Slalom style: Smooooothly does it. When you are just starting out, the best technique is to brake into the turn and then ease off the stoppers as you apex it, letting the bike roll through. Most courses are on grass with its associated traction problems, but grass is pretty nice stuff to fall on. As your skills improve, you will find yourself leaning the bike more, shifting your weight around and dabbing with the foot to get you down the track faster.

The thrills and spills of dual slalom make it one of mountain biking's most popular spectator disciplines.

Bike tweaks:

■ Suspension forks are great for dual slalom, but a rigid rear end is preferable to full suspension as you can accelerate faster.

■ Handlebar: Wide, high bars give you much better turning control.

■ Tyres: Tyre choice is very much dependent on your riding style; you may want to carve turns with your front tyre and drift out the back. Experiment.

■ Saddle: Lower your regular one a couple of inches to get it out of the way when you are cornering.

■ Pedals: Bear traps are much easier to get in and out of than clipless systems like SPuDs. As you get faster, the need to dab will probably increase.

C H A P T E R   8

advanced
technique

SPEED CORNERING, HOPPING,

JUMPING, DROP-OFFS, CLIMBING,

FLYING AND OTT STYLIN'

Paul Smith is a superb bike handler and trick rider. He is also an engineer apt to use mathematical formulae to show why a technique works at the slightest opportunity. Don't worry, I haven't given him the slightest opportunity.

If you've been reading what Justin and Jason have been saying about high performance riding, you'll have realised that the basic techniques we gave you in Chapter 3 just aren't going to cut it at that level. When you've ridden a lot, pushed your limits out a tad and are beginning to really hammer then you're ready to move up a level. So how do you learn this advanced stuff?

I've taught a lot of masterclasses for *MBUK* and I'm always amazed how quickly a skilled rider can help someone master a technique he or she has been sweating over for months.

Usually, when someone's really been trying to improve, they know what they should be doing and think they are doing it. What we do to produce almost instant success is tell them they're not doing it. It's very difficult to know exactly where your weight is, or whatever, on a bike, while concentrating on all the other things you have to handle to get through a difficult section.

For example, take a rider who has trouble with radical downhill sections. He knows he's got to get his weight back, thinks he's getting his weight back, but is actually taking impromptu flying lessons over the bars just the same. So the big shot teacher just has to give him the feeling of where his weight ought to be and the problem's solved.

A personal tutor is the best solution, and you'll find plenty of good riders prepared to take the time to help you if you ask. The next best thing is to watch yourself in action through video or pictures and compare what you're doing in practice with what you should be doing in theory.

Find out what you should be doing, why and what it looks like from the following words and pictures, compare it with what you are doing and go try again. Don't give up. You only have to get it right once and you'll get the feeling for the thing which you can build on, develop and improve.

Once you get used to pushing the limits of traction and gravity, pulling this kind of move won't be any skin off your nose.

SPEED CORNERING

Tyres, confidence, technique and practice are the main ingredients here. Find a good open corner with plenty of run out and ride round the thing as fast as you dare, experimenting with tyre pressures systematically as you practise.

THE TRICK: Extreme cornering usually requires the inside foot to be off the pedal and hanging above the ground for two reasons:

■ To provide an adjustable shift of centre of gravity down and towards the inside of the turn.
■ To slam on the floor and haul the bike back up if it starts to wash out away from you. A quick dab is usually enough to rescue you and the bike – it often results in a squiggly line on exit but that's better than a wash-out grinder crash.

1. The approach: Going into the corner looking for a good line through it and eyeing the exit to see where you can get back on the gas. Braking should be left as late as possible, but try to get it all under control before the corner really starts.

2. The lean: Starting to lean – the bike leans under you and your upper body leans a lot less. The faster you go, the more you have to lean the bike – if your body leant at the same angle, things would wash out and go wrong a lot sooner, so lean the bike and keep your upper body at more or less one third the lean of the bike. Oh, and don't forget to lift the inside pedal.

3. On the edge: Full lean and things should be on the move here. A bit of tyre scrub shows you're getting close to the limits, and a full on drift means you're about to go past them. Foot out just in case and fix your eyes on the exit point where you'll be flicking the bike back upright and hitting the cranks to power out.

Rob Warner knows the limits of his tyres like you know your mother's face.

4. The exit: If possible take a good wide exit and get the bike upright and in a straight line as quick as you can while starting to crank some power down. Pay attention to what comes next, power the pedals and wonder how you're going to keep this up as you're having difficulty breathing already.

THE BUNNY HOP

This little jump technique can help you overcome minor trail obstacles and forms the basis of a number of more difficult jump techniques.

1. Wheel up: As you approach the obstacle, squat down slightly on the bike. Pull your front wheel up using your arms and upper body.

2. Bounce: When your front wheel is at the height you want to bunny hop, bounce up using your ready 'cocked' legs, at the same time pushing forward on the bar.

3. Twist: Twist your grips forward as you do this to bring the back wheel up and over the obstacle.

4. Landing: To land, simply push down with your legs and compress them like springs as you land.

JUMPING

Jumping is cool. Here's a look at jumping for those who either haven't got their wheels off the ground yet or are having a hard time getting high and landing smooth.

1. The squat: Approach the jump at a speed you feel safe at (but fast enough to clear the jump) and squat down slightly on the bike as you begin to ride up the face of the jump.

2. The leap: As the front wheel reaches the top you should be starting to spring upwards while pulling up and slightly backwards on the bar, but keeping your body level.

Pull with your arms as opposed to leaning backwards – that's the mistake a lot of newbie jumpers make.

3. Flight: Just as the rear wheel leaves the jump, allow the rear of the bike to come up and forward underneath you as you straighten your arms slightly. Stay relaxed and things will fly smooth and straight. Tense up and gravity will have its way with you and dump you where it hurts.

4. The landing: Eye the landing spot and get ready to use your arms and legs as suspension. Extend your legs ready to allow them to compress as you touch down. When your wheels hit, you come down on to the bike, and that's when you bend your legs and arms to cushion the shock.

THE SPEED-JUMP

Despite its name, this is an anti-jump technique, designed to keep your wheels on the ground – you can't transmit power with your wheels in the air. Doing this at high speed is tricky; start small and work up.

1. Powering in: Concentrate on the crest of the jump from quite a way back and keep the power on. As you get closer, start to raise your upper body, ready to pull up on the bar.

2. The lift: Lift the front wheel, aiming to bring it down on the backside of the jump. As the front wheel lifts, keep your upper body up and get ready for the back of the bike to come up underneath your legs.

3. The thrust: As the rear wheel rides up the jump, let the bike lead you over the hump by straightening your arms and letting the rear come up under you, with the seat somewhere near your chest/stomach area. Pedalling is optional, but desirable.

4. Power out: As the bike starts to roll down the rear side of the jump, come forward and get back on the power.

THE PRE-JUMP

Hitting the crest of a hill at speed flings the bike and rider into the air for quite a distance which, if the ground is dropping away sharply under you, means you'll come down hard. When the ground drops away there is only one thing to do – alter your trajectory before the laws of physics do it for you.

1. The hop: Some distance back from the crest of the hill get ready to bunny hop. What you are aiming to do is time your bunny hop so as to land it on the downside of the hill you are pre-jumping.

2. Go for it: Once the bunny hop is under way you are fully committed. There's no going back!

3. Coming in to land: As you come down you can time your landing, either pushing the bike down to the ground to get down quicker or lifting it up under you to prolong your flight. The adjustment will only be a few inches, but it can make the difference between catching your rear wheel on the crest and flipping over the bars, missing the slope and landing heavily at the bottom, or the perfect touchdown.

4. Touchdown: The landing should be smooth and controlled, leaving you ready for what comes next and a yard in front of your dumbfounded mates.

STEEP CLIMBS

Long climbs are mostly a mental and physical thing, just keeping going until you're over; it's the steep stuff that usually causes problems with technique.

1. Balance point: On steep climbs your body weight has to do two things: keep the back tyre gripping and pushing the bike forward (retaining traction) and keep the front wheel on the ground, so you can steer and don't flip over backwards. You have to compromise. As you start to climb you'll find that there is a balance point where the front wheel doesn't lift and the rear doesn't spin – move your upper body forwards or backwards to keep the balance.

3. Smooth on the power: If you have to stand out of the saddle, try not to wag the bike from side to side too much, this usually upsets traction and balance. Keeping a smooth pedal stroke is even more important when standing. You're using your body weight to drive the cranks and that tends to produce sudden pulses of power. Don't let it. Sudden pulses of power will break traction and the rear wheel will spin or, if there's enough grip, the front wheel will lift.

2. Forward and back: On steeper stuff it's better to stay in the saddle if you can, standing usually results in a loss of traction. Come forward on the seat and pull backwards on the bar – not back and up. Remember, the bike is at an angle, so to make sure you pull back not up, imagine you're pulling the bar towards the seat clamp. Drop your upper body forwards and down and keep a smooth, even pedal stroke, turning circles not stomping up and down.

Hill climbing

To come down you have to go up, and although some people think going up isn't quite as much fun as coming down, there's no reason why it shouldn't be if you learn to do it well.

Long climbs: OK, on long climbs you need legs of steel and lungs the size of wildebeest to be really good. Correct training (see Chapter 5), will supply this within the limits of your natural physical ability. If you've done the right things physically, add the following:

A good mental attitude. Looking up the hill and thinking 'Oh no... It still goes up, I've had it' is the worst thing you can do. Tell yourself that everybody hurts on hills, it's not just you. Remember you've done the training and you're good. If someone passes you then tell yourself the extra effort will make that rider blow up later and you'll get him then...

If you've done everything to improve your climbing and it's not your strong point, there are some things you can do. Like getting ahead before the hill so you can set the pace.

If it's too wide for that, don't get sucked into a chase you can't handle. Ride your own race and leave yourself something in reserve for the later stages.

Ride over the top of the hill. It's near the top that you psyche out the rest. Get out of the saddle, go up a few cogs and really hammer over the crest. Tired riders aim for the top and relax as they reach their goal. Aim for half way down the other side and you can jump them by so much they won't chase.

Keep a steady rhythm. Concentrate on your pedal stroke – just as with the basic techniques, you should be pedalling circles rather than stomping up and down.

Over the top: Keep things going and keep it smooth over the top of the hill, too many failed hill climbs happen right as you go over the crest. Don't ease off the effort either, as with long climbs, power over the top and down the other side.

DROP-OFFS

There are two distinct techniques for handling drop-offs, depending on the speed at which you take them and how high they are:

1, 2 & 3. At low speeds, on smaller drop-offs and those with the right sort of run-out, you can simply get your weight a long way back, release the front brake and let the bike roll through the problem.

If the run-out isn't right, which means it's full of big lumps of rock, or the ground is shaped to grab the wheel rather than let it roll, then another technique is needed, like that used for bigger drops.

On bigger drop offs, from a couple of feet high, things start to get interesting. The technique is simple, a brief tug on the bars and a small wheelie will get the front wheel up in the air and provide you with a safe and controllable drop.

1. Get it up: Approaching the edge of the drop, start thinking about lifting the front wheel a foot or so in the air. Cover the rear brake at all times. Use one or two fingers – however many you feel comfortable with while gripping the bar firmly enough to wheelie.

BIGGER DROP-OFFS

2. Launch: Lift the front wheel as it gets to the edge and, giving a controlled burst on the pedals, take sight of your desired landing spot and get ready for the rear wheel to start dropping off the edge.

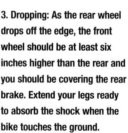

3. Dropping: As the rear wheel drops off the edge, the front wheel should be at least six inches higher than the rear and you should be covering the rear brake. Extend your legs ready to absorb the shock when the bike touches the ground.

4. Landing: On most drop-offs a rear wheel first landing is desirable, often with the rear brake on to prevent the bike from either slamming the front wheel down or looping over backwards. As you touch down, bend your legs to soften the impact and lean forward as the front wheel comes down, releasing the rear brake as it does.

DOWNHILL PERCENTAGES

When you start downhilling you struggle to learn the techniques that will make you go faster and faster. It's only when you're really fast you start to play the percentages. That means going faster where you're going too slow and slower where you're going too fast. Going too slow: At the start and on the flat.

1. Fast start: Get up to speed as soon as possible. Sauntering away from the start line costs seconds, and a few seconds can mean a lot of places up, or down, the time sheets.

2. Flying the flat: Even when legs and lungs tell you otherwise, keeping the speed up in the flatter sections matters a heap.

■ Make yourself small and aerodynamic, reducing wind resistance.

■ Push it as hard as you sensibly can – how hard you try depends whereabouts you are on the course, it's no use blowing up in the first third of the downhill. Time your effort for the sections where it really makes a difference.

Going too fast: When you're fast enough to place high, finishing matters. You're probably going too fast in the corners and on gnarly terrain.

3. Don't stack: Corners are a good place to make up time on less experienced riders, but if there is a high risk on a certain corner take it well within your limits – remember, to finish first you have to finish.

4. Don't get too sketchy: Calm down! Stay as smooth and unflustered as possible in technical sections. If you're unsure of something then slow down and ride within your limits, remember in a downhill race when the adrenalin is flowing, you are probably hitting things a good five or even ten miles per hour faster than in practice and getting at least a few feet off line. There are times, when micro seconds are in it, that you're going to have to charge like a nutter on technical sections. When your adrenalin and confidence is high it often works, but don't try to force it.

OVER THE TOP

Posing, jumping, styling and just plain showing off are a big part of the pleasure you get from bike-handling skills. Some people say you shouldn't show off. Why not? In any form of entertainment it's the show-offs who provide the buzz – and the mega laffs when they get it wrong!

I mean showing off your skills, of course; cruising around the campsite at the races with a bike worth more than the car you arrived in and cleaner than a very clean thing simply sucks!

Showing off, posing, styling, means doing something very few people can do, and being as calm and understated about it as you possibly can.

Here are a few tricks that look good, but aren't that hard really:

The trackstand

The first thing you learn about bikes is that they fall over if they aren't moving. But that's not true. Keeping your bike still on the spot without

taking your feet from the pedals is fairly easy once you get the hang of it, and the pose factor is way high. I mean, imagine being able to stop and have a chat with someone with no need to put a foot down. Especially when you've got it so sussed you can stand still with the minimum of wobbling and bar turning.

Here's how:

■ To start with, find a slight hill and point your bike up it with the rear brake on, turn the bars forty five degrees or so in whichever direction you like the most and put some pressure on the front pedal. Let go of the brake and still with one foot on the floor get a feeling for how you can let the bike roll under you or be pushed up the hill away from you by pedal pressure alone.

■ Once you get the hang of things, start to lift your foot from the ground and on to the pedal (either sitting or standing – although standing is easier to start with). You'll be able to keep your foot on the pedal longer as you get it sussed. When you've mastered it you should be able to ride to a standstill on the flat, balance, and ride off using a combination of pedal input and bar turning.

■ That's the basic trackstand. Now learn it sitting down, and then with no hands – that's way cool and is the top pose for checking out race result sheets!

Wheelies

Wheelies aren't really that difficult, you've just got to get a feel for them. The trick is to start small and build up, it's no use trying to master coasting wheelies down your nearest hill until you can get the front wheel off the ground confidently.

One thing to remember – SPDs or toe straps will hinder first time learners, so either don't clip/strap in, or use flat pedals. Speedy foot removal is essential in the (very) likely event of a mishap. Try it this way:

■ Riding at a reasonably slow pace (near the top of the block in the middle chainring), drop your upper body weight forward and slightly down, bending at the elbows.

■ Straighten up quickly, push hard on the pedal and pull upwards on the bars to lift the front wheel. You are trying to get the rear wheel to come underneath you, rather than lift the front wheel, but you must get the balance point right. Lean back and let the rear wheel roll under you slightly.

■ If (when) things start to go too far, a quick pull on the rear brake will bring the front end down to the ground or, once you get better at it, back to the balance point.

■ Once you're good enough to get a couple of pedal revolutions in, use the rear brake to control your speed, otherwise you'll end up going faster and faster.

Hans 'No Way' Rey knows all the moves.

Packing this much style into a jump is hard even for a good bike handler but it shows you what is possible if you can look pain in the eye.

Stylin' jumps

Jumping – or the anti jump speed-jumps and pre-jumps – is a bow in the mountain biker's quiver of advanced riding techniques, but it's also the classic pose and demon psyche out.

Imagine you're hacking in the middle of a cross-country race and you come to a section of tree roots – every other shaven legged boring biker is braking and rattling, but you jump it.

A quick bounce out of the first root and you and your bike are a couple of feet in the air, styling it over the rest of the roots, aiming for a silky smooth touchdown in front of the eye-rattling shakers who rode the section.

The basic jump isn't that styling though. The trick is to make it look as easy as possible – but to appear that cool you have to be able to click out a stylish jump without even thinking about it.

Try a slight lean of the bike and twist of the bars, coupled with a smoother, more controlled style to give the impression of a seasoned air bandit.

One handers are a simple yet good-looking variation, and lofting a one-hander while pointing to the photographers always gets attention in the right places.

Start by opening your fingers on the grip while jumping and build up, lifting your hand further and further away until you get confident and know exactly how long you can leave it before having to get your hand back on the bar.

Smile for the camera.

Being able to pop a half decent wheelie is enough for most folks.

C H A P T E R   9

advanced
equipment

BETTER BIKES, WHAT TO LOOK

FOR, WHAT YOU'RE PAYING FOR,

FULL SUSPENSION, UPGRADES

It's when you've got your technique sorted and begin riding closer to the limit that you start finding things your bike could do better. If you're buying the magazines too, you'll see the stream of new after-market components designed to help it do just that. Do they work? Well, as Brant said in Chapter 2, some of them do, some of them don't. This chapter's to help you decide what you really need to improve your riding.

But first things first. If you've bought a basic entry level bike you'll probably not be thinking of adding bits to it. Only when it has taught you all it can will you be thinking of changing it. The upgrade most people make when they're good enough to need improved performance is to buy a new bike.

Which new bike?
Of course, improved performance depends entirely on what you do with your bike. Different riders need different things.

Here, as an example, are what three common types of rider will be looking for in a new scoot and the type of machine that they might go for (or what I would go for if I was them).

CROSS-COUNTRY RACER
After a season climbing up the cross-country placings, the serious racer will usually be looking for:
⚙ Better, lighter frame
⚙ Better, lighter wheels
⚙ Better componentry
In mountain bikes, better and lighter means expensive. Here are some options:

Better, lighter frame
You've got three frame materials to consider:

Steel can be light and strong, but some lightweight steel frames are just too flexible for their own good. When you've test ridden a few you'll find a frame that balances the forgiving characteristics of steel with a point and squirt style handling package. But lightweight steel will always have that extra flex. You may prefer it, or you may resent it soaking up power.

Aluminium is the opposite. The feeling of power transmission you get from a good aluminium frame is what attracts riders. They have a

seemingly explosive sprinting and climbing ability which lightweight steel frames struggle to match – but remember that fatigue plays a big part in your performance, and there is no denying that aluminium offers the harsher ride.

Titanium offers just about the best of both worlds but it costs big bucks. A typical titanium frame weighs just about the same as aluminium and yet offers the riding qualities of steel. In the last few years more thought has been devoted to designing the frame for the material being used. A good titanium frame is a joy to ride and will last for years; the downside is that they do cost a packet.

Better, lighter wheels
A good wheel package is essential, and lighter tyres with your preferred tread and lighter inner tubes can be added later.

Better componentry
Easy, you just pay more and you're looking at Shimano Deore XT or XTR.

Typical solution
The race head would go for something like the bike pictured above, with a quality frame and componentry to match.

Rich racer solution – the Kona Hei Hei. The racehead would probably go for something like this. A quality responsive titanium frame with a well sorted component package and handling to shame nearly all other bikes out there. But at a cost.

DOWNHILLER
Constant good placings at the year's downhill races will leave up-and-comers looking for the equipment to take them closer to the top, and with suspension being the name of the game, here's what to look for:

- ⚙ Good, solid components
- ⚙ Bombproof wheels
- ⚙ A balanced suspension package
- ⚙ Easy to service/parts availability

Good, solid components
A good, tough steel frame is a wise choice, with high quality, strong components. You're not looking for light bars and stems for downhill, you're looking for the strongest available.

Bombproof wheels
As Jason says in Chapter 7, strong hand-built wheels take one element of worry out of the downhiller's day.

Suspension

You have two choices, do it by halves, with front suspension and a rigid rear, or go the whole hog with full suspension:

Front suspension only is still a viable option, especially if you're limiting yourself to the British races, where most of the courses feature more pedalling on relatively smooth surfaces than technical riding through the rough stuff.

Beware of having too long a travel fork on the front of rigid frames as this screws up the handling. You're better off buying forks with less travel but better quality action.

Full suspension is getting more and more popular and sorted, but you still have to choose between systems which lock out under load and those which remain active (see Full Suspension below).

Active suspension bikes are much more suited to downhill racing as the suspension still works – to a greater or lesser degree depending upon design – under pedalling and drive loads.

Sprinting over fist-sized rocks is more than possible with some of the longer travel bikes, something you would be hard pushed to do at all on a rigid bike, let alone at anywhere near the same speed.

Easy to service

Pivot maintenance and shock servicing has to be taken into account, and serviceability should rank high on your list of priorities unless you're a chronic bike fettler.

The rising downhiller would probably go for a more active design like this, with reasonably low maintenance requirements (though with no damping system to control the elastomer springs).

Typical solution

The Pro-flex 955, pictured above, would be one solution for a rising downhiller.

FUN RIDER

OK, so you don't really hammer the cross-country or downhill circuits, you ride just for the fun of it. Basically, you just need a bike which will last you a while, is comfortable, and doesn't cost the earth to maintain. You'll be looking for:

- Lightish frame
- Good components
- Good handling
- Well specced wheels

Lightish frame

A fully rigid steel framed bike is a cool place to start as you can simply add to it later when you have settled more into the type of riding that you want to do. Things to look out for are quality welding and componentry and a sturdy set of wheels.

Good components

In most cases you put your money down and go up a notch or two on the Shimano groupset ladder.

Good handling

Suspension used to have an adverse effect on handling. Not so now; better sorted forks steer pretty much as well as the average rigid fork, and more bikes are coming out with front suspension or have it as an option.

Steering, braking and comfort are all improved, and no longer do you get those numb wrists after a couple of hours' rough riding. What's more, you can see where you're going on those really bumpy descents – but you pay for it in added weight and a bigger price tag.

Typical solution

Something like the bike in the picture above would suit you fine.

FULL SUSPENSION

Like Brant said in Chapter 2, full suspension is the future of mountain biking. The ultimate full suspension mountain bike for every rider is yet to be made, but full suspension is fairly sorted now; the logic is undeniable, getting it right on the bike was the problem.

It's all simple enough in theory. When a bike hits a bump it has to go

Singletrack solution: Depends on your favourite riding, I reckon the singletrack fanatic would go for something like this, for its nimble handling and good component choice.

upwards. A bike and rider is a lot of mass to fling into the air violently and come down hard. But if we isolate the wheels from the rest of the bike using springs, only the much lighter wheels have to move upwards to clear the bump, leaving the rest of the bike more or less unaffected.

Letting the wheel move out of the way instead of the whole bike is a more efficient way of covering ground, but what are the pros and cons?

Pros
- ✿ Greater traction, for braking, accelerating and cornering (the springs also push the wheels down on to the ground)
- ✿ Increased comfort levels
- ✿ Increased speeds

Cons
- ✿ Extra weight
- ✿ Sometimes complex mechanicals need servicing more often
- ✿ Prices are high
- ✿ Poor designs sap rider energy

TWO SYSTEMS

There are two ways of making full suspension work on a mountain bike;

SUSPENSION

Suspension isolates the wheels from the rest of the bike, separating it into two bits of mass (two separate lumps of weight):

Sprung mass: the parts supported by springs (the frame and associated parts and the rider)

Unsprung mass: the parts not supported by springs (wheels, fork sliders, brakes and some of the swingarm)

it's either designed to effectively lock out under hard pedalling loads or to work all the time (active or full floating suspension).

Lock-out suspension makes the machine feel more like a rigid bike in the sprints, which suits new users. The downside is that it takes energy to extend the suspension to lock-out point, energy which should be driving the rear wheel. So, although they may give you the impression they're faster, they may well not be – the proof is in the stopwatch, not what a rider feels.

Active suspension is affected as little as possible by load. To use it effectively, your riding style has to be changed a little, but not drastically. You need to ride more smoothly. Sprints have to be a little less aggro, and you spend more time sitting down putting effort into pedalling rather than standing up using your body weight.

DO I NEED IT?

You need it if:

- ❂ You want better traction, going up, coming down, and going around
- ❂ You like going fast, comfortably
- ❂ You can adapt to riding smoothly

SUSPENSION FORKS

Dissipating and delaying the transfer of bumps from the wheel to the rest of the bike is the main aim of suspension forks too. There are lots of them on the market, using different methods (which we discussed in Chapter 2) to do this. So what's what?

Fork types

There are two main types of suspension fork: telescopic and linkage design.

Telescopic forks either have the lower legs sliding up and down with the wheel over the upper legs (Manitou, Marzocchi, Rock Shox and so on) or work the other way up, with the lower legs sliding within the upper legs (Halson Inversion, Mountain Cycle Suspenders).

Linkage forks either have linkages between the bike and two long fork

Rock Shox Mag 21 forks lead the way in air/oil shock performance.

legs (Girvin Vector, Quasar Linx), or between the fork legs and the wheel (Lawwill Leader).

Telescopic forks are easier to make, they're just four tubes, four bushes, some seals, and whatever the manufacturer chooses to put inside them to do the springing and the damping. Linkage forks are harder to make because tolerances at the bushes must be near perfect. Any play will be amplified because of the length of the linkages, and excessive play will be felt when steering.

Both systems try to accomplish the same thing, with differing results.

The idea is to dissipate bump force as heat in the spring and damping media, transferring what's left to the bike over a longer period of time which makes it less violent. The perfect suspension system does this just as well for small hits as for big ones, gets the wheel back down quickly to deal with the next hit, deals with that equally well and keeps the wheels on the ground over dips and bumps for better traction.

That's the Holy Grail. In practice, all systems do some of these things better than others and you have to choose which best suits your style.

DO I NEED SUSPENSION FORKS?

Yup, you need them if:

- ❂ You want to ride faster and/or safer
- ❂ You want increased comfort/traction
- ❂ You like doing big jumps but can't afford new rigid forks every week.

Justin Loretz finds out what 3in of suspension travel will allow you to do.

UPGRADES

I've talked a lot about suspension because it is the new thing in mountain biking; it's not the first priority but you may be thinking about getting it. There is a lot of kit out there, so what should you go for first?

Tyres

If you're starting from a stock bike then this is the best place to begin upgrading. Replacing the stock tyres with lighter Kevlar-beaded versions lightens the bike and, better still, loses a bit of rotating mass too. Less rotating mass makes it easier to turn the wheels. Try it, you'll feel as though you've dropped a load of weight off the bike when in fact you've lost half a pound or so at most.

Changing to lighter tyres gives you a choice of tread pattern so choose tyres that work for you in the conditions you ride. Take the advice of local shops and riders who ride the same places you do.

These are the basics of tread pattern application:

Mud tyre: A tall, open tread works well for mud, and it helps if the tyre is narrow, to prevent excessive build-up of mud around the frame.

Directional tyres: Designed specifically for the front, these do a better job of steering and braking.

Dry tyres: A closer, shallower tread works well in the dry, combined with a more rounded shape to the tyre for slightly less rolling resistance and good cornering grip.

All rounders: Good, all round tyres usually have medium height, open-spaced tread patterns and respond well to changes in pressure. Use low

Suspension places added demand on your tyres. Choose treads carefully.

The Panaracer Smoke is a good tyre for muddy conditions.

As its names suggests, Specilized's Hardpack is a good tyre when the going's dry.

Panaracer's Dart is a directional tyre.

You can't go wrong with Specilized's Ground Control tyre as an all rounder.

The Flite saddle is one of the most popular aftermarket upgrades to any bike.

Clipless pedal systems increase your pedalling efficiency.

Speed demons need disc brakes (above). These are the future of braking on performance mountain bikes. Bar ends (left) allow you to use larger muscle groups when climbing. Downhillers prefer a higher bar position than cross-country riders, hence the advent of curvy bars (below).

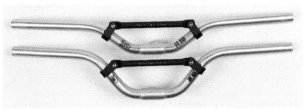

pressure for the slippery stuff and higher pressure when the ground starts to dry out.

Bar ends

There are three main types: stubbies, short bend and long bend. Bar ends give another hand position which can be better for climbing or just somewhere different to put tired hands.

Clipless pedals

One of the most popular upgrades is a switch from toe-clips and straps to clipless pedals. Shimano tended to dominate the market for a while with the SPD system, but onZa, Tioga, Ritchey, VP, Look, Time and so on have been quick to catch up. You'll need compatible shoes too.

If you ride hard and keep losing your chain, fit a DCD chain tensioner and keep on riding.

Saddle

There are quite a few lightweight saddles on the market, but by far the most popular is the Selle Italia Flite. A leather seat cut down to just about

the bare minimum with titanium rails makes a comfortable yet light alternative to the 'heavyweight steel-railed saddle from hell' found on most off the shelf bikes.

Women often find the seat that comes with most bikes is too narrow, too long and none too comfy. There is now a good selection of seats specifically designed for women by women, most of which are also available in a lightweight version (see Chapter 4).

DOWNHILL EQUIPMENT

Chain tensioners: Devices designed to prevent the chain coming off. Either a roller system hung on the chainstay or a sprung system to provide extra chain tension to the rear mech.

Wide bars: For downhill/dual slalom, wider handlebars offer more control and a more aggressive riding stance.

Disc brakes: These give immense stopping power in the wet or dry, usually requiring only one finger at the lever to work them no matter what the speed.

CHAPTER 10

the dirty bit

MONEY-SAVING MAINTENANCE,

ESSENTIAL REPAIRS AND

ADJUSTMENTS, GEARS, MECHS

AND BRAKES

Every best selling book needs a dirty bit and this is ours. Keeping your bike in excellent condition saves you loads of money and heaps of frustration in the long run, but you do have to get your hands dirty. A lot and often.

Hammering a bunch of tubes, gears, pulleys and bearings through the grinding paste that we call mud takes its toll. Everything takes a beating, the frame, the wheels and the components. To get the most miles out of your components and ensure your own safety, you need to examine your frame, bars and stem regularly for signs of damage, check your wheels are true, adjust brakes and gear mechs and clean and lubricate the moving parts.

If you're rich and short of time, the local bike shop can do much of this for you – it makes sense to let them do the bigger jobs. But mountain bikers don't really see things that way. Because we need to be able to fix our machinery out on the trail (or slap together a 'get you home bodge') it makes sense to do the basic maintenance work too. You only find your way around your equipment by working on it.

At the very least, a weekly clean, lube and inspection session will keep

those expensive components from wearing out too fast and cut down the time your bike spends in the local workshop.

How much can I do?
Most of it, if you have the time and inclination. Some people glitch any mechanical object they touch, you know the type – the whole thing springs apart, the bearings roll down the drain the minute they look at it. If that's you, just do the basic maintenance and give thanks for bike shops. But if you're reasonably ept (opposite of inept, I say) replacing most of the major bearings and components is within your grasp. Bicycles are pretty simple things, once you get the feel for them and have the right tools and information.

More information
We're unable to give you that level of detailed information here, a complete guide to mountain bike maintenance and repair would be a book to itself. And it so happens I've written it. It's called *GRIME TIME* and it's published by Future Books. If you want to get heavily into mechanicing,

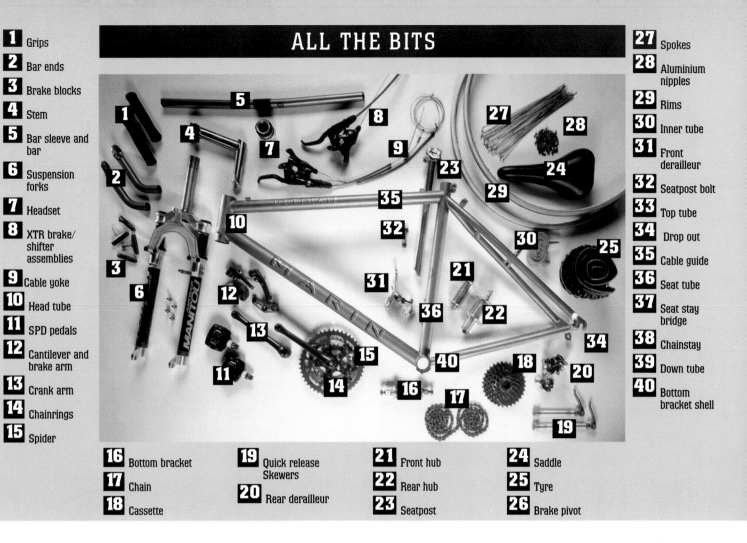

1 Grips
2 Bar ends
3 Brake blocks
4 Stem
5 Bar sleeve and bar
6 Suspension forks
7 Headset
8 XTR brake/shifter assemblies
9 Cable yoke
10 Head tube
11 SPD pedals
12 Cantilever and brake arm
13 Crank arm
14 Chainrings
15 Spider
16 Bottom bracket
17 Chain
18 Cassette
19 Quick release Skewers
20 Rear derailleur
21 Front hub
22 Rear hub
23 Seatpost
24 Saddle
25 Tyre
26 Brake pivot
27 Spokes
28 Aluminium nipples
29 Rims
30 Inner tube
31 Front derailleur
32 Seatpost bolt
33 Top tube
34 Drop out
35 Cable guide
36 Seat tube
37 Seat stay bridge
38 Chainstay
39 Down tube
40 Bottom bracket shell

get hold of a copy. What I'm going to do here is look at the adjustments and replacements you're most likely to want a quick reference to.

Mountain bike maintenance

When you use your bike a lot it's tempting to leave cleaning it until it really needs it. There's even some cred in having a muddy bike that shows you really ride. We have some people on the *MBUK* staff who take that attitude – or seem to; it's only when you look further that you find the working bits are beautifully clean and lubed.

Those of us who are engineers and have a working knowledge of the damage bits of grit can do to bearings, tend to clean and lube more often.

I reckon it's best to give everything a wipe down after every ride, clean and lube the chain once a week, checking the brake blocks and cables and give it a thorough clean and check over every couple of weeks.

Cleaning

A couple of buckets of water, a stiff brush and a water dispersing lubricant (WD 40 is commonly available) is all you need.

Hoses save time, but they can also cause damage. A garden hose is fine so long as you don't goosh water directly at the seals of bearings like the hubs and bottom bracket.

Try not to get any water inside the tubes – go easy where the seatpost

and stem enter the frame, for example.

Once it's dry, a quick squirt of water-dispersing lube on the chain (keep the spray in one place and turn the pedals backwards to move the chain), down the seat tube, up the steerer tube along exposed lengths of cables and so on, will keep corrosion at bay.

Chain job

■ Wipe the chain with a cloth soaked in one of the many available cleaning solvents. Keep the solvent off the tyre, rim, hub and bottom bracket. Spray the chain and leave for five minutes.

■ Spray the chain again and scrub out all the links with an old toothbrush. If you're using a water soluble solvent goosh out the gunge with a hose.

■ You'll probably have to do it again to get it really clean.

■ Wipe the chain with a clean dry rag – hold the rag around it and turn a pedal backwards. Leave to dry.

■ Lube sparingly. Too much attracts dirt. With spray lube, hold the can still and turn a pedal backwards to carry the chain under the spray. With non spray lube put a drop on every roller. Leave to soak in for five minutes before spinning the cranks.

Take my tip: If you ride a lot, invest in a chain cleaner. It's a receptacle for solvent with a built-in brush arrangement that cleans chains better and

---

quicker. Just fill as instructed, clamp around the chain and turn a pedal backwards. Excellent.

Heavy duty lube

There are all sorts of lube on offer, some are light, pick up little dirt, but need replacing every ride. Others are heavier, last longer, but pick up the crud.

For heavy duty work it's become common to apply a 'dry' lube (usually teflon-based) and leave it to soak in, then apply a 'wet' lube over the top. The idea is that the dry lube sits inside the rollers while the wet lube keeps water out.

Finish Line produce two good lubes designed to be used this way.

Check-up

Make sure:
- Nothing is bent or broken.
- There are no frayed cables.
- Your wheels are true and the spokes properly tensioned by 'pinging' them with a fingernail. If they produce the same note they're evenly tensioned. On the back wheel the spokes on the mech side will give a different note to those the other side. In this case they should be the same as the others on that one side.
- Examine the frame joints for cracks, discolouring of the paint, crazing of the paint or dark marks under the paint which indicate that the metal has distorted in some way. On steel bikes, pay great attention to the most sensitive area where the head tube meets the top and down tubes.

Examine your stem and bars too. The danger areas are where the tube goes into a clamp of any sort, including the area under the lever clamps.

ESSENTIAL REPAIRS AND ADJUSTMENTS

Fixing a flat with two levers

1 If you have a reasonably tight tyre then you'll need two tyre levers to get it off. Push both levers under the tyre's bead roughly six inches apart. Don't lever the first one and then try to get the

---

THE TOOLS YOU'LL NEED

For general weekly maintenance, the following will do the job:
- **2, 2.5, 3, 4, 5, 6 and 8mm allen keys**
- **8, 9, 10, 11mm spanners (combination – open end and ring)**
- **Phillips No 2 screwdriver**
- **Small pliers**
- **Cable cutters (it's worth buying high quality cutters)**
- **Chain tool (to suit narrow chains)**
- **Two tyre levers**
- **Puncture kit**
- **Pump**
- **Chain cleaning tool**
- **Degreaser**
- **Chain lubricant**
- **Grease**

This will allow you to adjust brake and gear systems, replace cables, change tyres and tubes, adjust bar and stem, seat and post, clean the chain and fit new brake pads. It's a good basic toolkit for tackling straightforward maintenance – leave the more complicated bottom bracket, headset and wheel jobs to your local bike shop.

The equipment you'll need for a full service is covered in the *GRIME TIME* book (see page 132).

---

second one under the bead because the tyre will be too tight to get the lever under it.

2 Pull the first lever down until it hooks around a spoke. Then pull on the second lever. You must put both levers under the tyre before you try to lift the bead upwards and over the rim. With some tyres it can be very difficult to get a second tyre lever in after you have hooked the first one over a spoke.

3 Gradually work around the tyre with the second lever, trying not to damage the tube too much. Really tight tyres may even need three tyre levers. If this is the case, always take off the tyre some distance away from easily offended people – mucho swearing and cursing often ensues.

THE TWO LEVER TECHNIQUE FOR REMOVING A TYRE

Changing the tube

1 Once one side of the tyre is off the rim, reach in and pull out the inner tube. Pull the tyre open and check inside for anything that might be protruding from the inner surface of the tyre – don't just look, run your fingers inside to check for thorns, and so on.

2 Inflate the tube until it just holds its shape. Only put enough air in to stop it from flopping around – this will make it much easier to fit into the tyre.

3 Push the valve through the hole in the rim and push the rest of the tube into the tyre. Try to push the tube well into the rim so that it won't get in the way of the bead when you push it back over the rim.

4 Push the valve inwards, away from the rim, as you begin to push the bead of the tyre over the rim. Try not to trap the tube near the valve – easily done, since this is the bulkiest section of the tube. Work around the tyre, pushing the bead back over the rim with your thumbs.

5 As you get to the last section of bead to be pushed back over the rim, things can start getting difficult. Make sure as much of the bead as possible is pushed into the well in the middle of the rim so that you are left with the maximum amount of slack at the tight section. Do not use the tyre levers to lever the last part back on to the rim! This could pinch the tube and puncture it again. Push the tyre hard with your thumbs, starting at the very end of the section of bead to be pushed back on. It often helps to hold one end still while you push the other end on, rather than trying to do both at the same time.

6 Inflate the tyre, checking along the way that the tyre is seated evenly on to the rim. Once you get about 10psi in the tyre, it is inflated enough to seat, but is still soft enough to be pushed around by hand to seat it properly. There is often a small ridge around the top of the bead that you can use as a reference to check if the tyre is seated correctly, by just spinning the wheel and watching the line in relation to the rim.

CHANGING THE TUBE

Chain jobs: The drive chain

A chain may not be the ideal way of transmitting force from the cranks to the rear wheel, but it's just about the only working method that is simple, cheap, lightweight, strong and easy to service. Once a chain gets worn, however, the life of the sprockets driven by that chain will be drastically reduced.

When a chain wears, the distance between the rollers that contact the teeth on the sprockets becomes greater. So instead of distributing the load over four or five teeth, it all goes on to the small contact patch between just one roller and a tooth. The rollers then begin to wear at an accelerated rate. So, in the long run, it pays to look after your chain and replace it as soon as signs of wear are visible.

Looking for wear in a chain can be difficult if you don't know what to look for, but there is one method we can use that only requires a good quality ruler. Measure the length of 12 full links (the distance between 25 pins). This distance should be 12in. A chain should be replaced when the 12 link length reaches 12.125in (an eighth of an inch longer).

Splitting and fitting a chain

1 To split a chain, run it through the ridge furthest away from the threaded driver end. Screw the driver up and seat it centrally on the pin. Then firmly screw in the driver until it pushes the pin out of the other side, taking care that the driver doesn't run off the pin and start bending the chain plates. With Shimano chains, you can push the pin all of the way out because a new special pin will be required to re-join the chain afterwards. Don't split the chain on one of the special pins because this will damage the link plate.

2 With regular chains, don't push the pin all the way out – it needs to be pushed back in again afterwards. Pull the chain out through the front and rear mech, make a note of how the chain is threaded through the rear mech if you've never done this before. To get your new chain to the same length lay it beside the old one and remove any surplus links.

SPLITTING AND FITTING A CHAIN

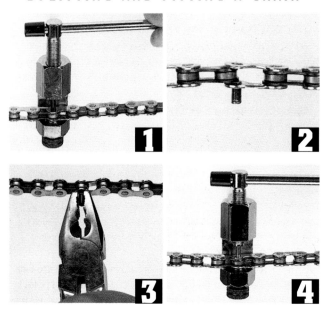

3   To fit the chain, thread it through the front mech first, around the rear sprocket and then drop it down through the rear mech. Do this on the smallest sprocket at the rear and don't loop the chain over the front chainring yet, the slackness you get doing it this way helps when pulling the two ends of the chain together.

On a Sedis chain, just push the pin back in with the chain tool until both ends of the pin just protrude from the link plates. With a Shimano chain you must use the special replacement pin (it's sold in packs of three). Don't try using the old pin because the chain will snap in a very short time. Push the pointed end of the special pin into the chain and then drive it in with the chain tool until the end is just sticking out from the link plate. Snap off the pointed end with pliers and check that the chain isn't stiff on that link.

4   If the link is stiff, flex the chain sideways in your hands or run it over the ridge on the chain tool closest to the threaded driver. Lightly press against the pin with the driver and then check the link again. Repeat until the link rotates freely.

The front mech or front derailleur

The modern front mech is a careful balance of high strength and low weight. The cage has to be strong enough to push the chain from chainring to chainring. The clamp has to be tight enough not to slip around the seat tube but, because frame tubes are getting thinner and thinner every year, it must also be designed so that it won't crush the seat tube. On top of this, there has to be some form of return spring

that is strong enough to pull the chain off the large chainring to a smaller one, yet light enough so the user can push against it when shifting to a bigger one.

All of this is squeezed into a few bits of alloy, a couple of pivots and a funny shaped steel cage. The job of a front mech is a simple one, but the front mech itself is more complicated than first meets the eye, and a few millimetres of adjustment here and there can make all the difference to its performance.

The two jobs you are most likely to tackle on a front mech are changing the cable and adjusting the mech. When you change a cable make sure that the outer cables are clean and have fresh lube squirted down them, wipe lube on the new inner cable before you push it through the outers, and make sure the cable stops are cleaned out prior to installation.

Replacing a cable

1   Set the gear shifter to the inner chainring position and undo the cable clamp bolt on the front mech. Pull the inner cable from the outers as you remove the outers from the frame (make note of what piece of outer went where on the frame and any guides or pulleys the inner went through). Remove the cable cover from the rear of the shifter (if fitted) and push the cable until the nipple pops out. Pull the cable all of the way out of the shifter.

2   Clean out the cable outers and spray them with light lube. Push the new cable through the shifter and replace any cable covers on the shifter. Thread the inner cable through the outers and replace them in their stops on the frame. Screw the barrel adjuster on the shifter all of the way in (clockwise) and then two full turns back out. Thread the inner cable

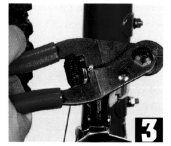

FRONT MECH:
REPLACING A
CABLE

FRONT MECH: ADJUSTMENT

through any guides or pulleys and then under the clamp bolt on the front mech. Pull the cable tight with either some pliers or a third hand tool and tighten the clamp bolt.

3 Trim the cable to length (leave about an inch) and fit a cable end cap. This makes the job look neat and tidy and also stops the cable fraying – frayed cables can catch on your calves.

Adjustment

1 To work properly the front mech outer cage plate should be 1-2mm above the big chainring. To adjust the height of the mech, undo (anti-clockwise) the clamp bolt on the main clamp that goes around the frame tube. The bolt will either be on the left-hand side of the bike for a 'hinge' type clamp or on the right-hand side of the mech alloy body for the 'endless band' type. If your chainrings aren't round then set the mech 1-2mm from the highest part of the ring.

2 The outer cage plate must be set parallel to the chainrings. Look down from above as you twist the mech on the frame tube, but be careful not to move the mech up or down because this will affect any adjustment you made in step 1. Some mechs move as you tighten the clamp bolt and this movement will have to be taken into account if the mech is to be correctly aligned when the bolt is tightened. A clamp bolt doesn't have to be mega tight, especially on thin-walled frame tubes. Tighten it just enough so that you can't move the mech when you try and rotate it with both hands. The only thing trying to move the front mech is cable tension, aside from that there is no other reason for the mech to move.

3 The limit screws adjust the point where the mech is physically stopped from moving. The outer screw controls the stop when shifting into the largest chainring and the inner screw does the inner chainring. If, after cable installation, you can't engage the large chainring, screw the limit screw anti-clockwise until you can. If the chain over-shifts and falls over the chainring on to the crank, screw the limit screw clockwise until it stops over-shifting.

If you can't engage the small chainring, screw the limit screw anti-clockwise until you can. If the chain over-shifts and falls over the chainring into the bottom bracket area, screw the limit screw clockwise until it stops over-shifting. If the limit screw is screwed all of the way out and you still can't engage the small chainring check that there isn't too much cable tension by turning the barrel adjuster on the shifter clockwise to decrease cable tension. You usually have to ride backwards and forwards carrying a screwdriver and re-adjusting until things are sorted. It can be done on a bike stand, but you'll usually find that the front mech shifts differently when under power.

4 To adjust an indexed front mech, shift into the middle ring and turn the barrel adjuster until the chain doesn't rub on the mech plates in any of the rear gears. Turn the adjuster clockwise to bring the cage closer to the frame, and anti-clockwise to bring it closer to the outer chainring.

The rear mech or rear derailleur

In design terms, a rear mech is something of a compromise. It's a collection of simple levers and two toothed wheels held in a flimsy cage, all pivoting on a bolt through the frame.

It has the job of pushing the chain from one cog to the next and does so using just cable or spring tension.

It's engineered just enough to do the job. By skimping on the depth of tooth profiles (so they wear faster) and messing around with the chain link profiles (which makes them weaker) the rest of the transmission system

EMERGENCY REPAIRS:

SNAPPED CABLE

A snapped cable is annoyingly hard to fix unless you carry a small electrical wire joiner (the type with a screw terminal each end of a plastic block) and an appropriate screwdriver. They're light, cheap and offer a good strong join when done up tight.

⚙ Once joined, the cable will be approximately 5mm too long. Unclamp the cable, pull it through and reclamp to the right length.

REAR MECH: CABLE REPLACEMENT

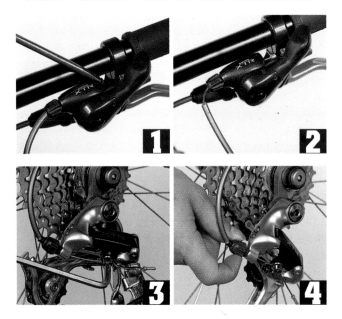

has been 'softened up' just enough to let a remarkably lightweight and simple rear mech do the job without breaking.

Bad shifting can often be traced to the cables and the rear derailleur alone is rarely the source of the problem. Over-shifting (where the chain is pushed past the largest sprocket into the wheel) or under-shifting (where the chain won't go on to the smallest sprocket) are easy to remedy, although if a bike starts to do this for no apparent reason there is a strong chance that the derailleur hanger (the part of the frame it screws on to) is bent, or the derailleur cage itself is bent.

Cable replacement

1 Change gear until the chain is on the smallest sprocket, then loosen the cable clamp bolt on the derailleur. Remove the end cap (if fitted) and pull the inner cable from the outer. Remove the outers from the frame and note which piece of outer came from which part of the bike.

2 On RapidFire shifters, pop out the small plug-in cover and push the cable inner until the nipple pops out of the hole (some old units have a small crosshead screw which holds a cover in place), then pull the cable out. Thumbshifters are much easier – just push the cable, grab the nipple and pull out the cable. Screw the barrel adjuster on the mech all of the way in (clockwise) and then one full turn out again. Do the same on the shifter but with two full turns out again.

3 Thread the new cable through the shifter and replace the plug-in cap (if fitted). Thread the inner through the outers and then slot the outers into their stops on the frame, making sure you have cleaned and

lubed the outers with degreaser and lube or WD40 before you re-insert the new inner wire. Check that the mech and chain are on the smallest sprocket then thread the inner through the rear mech. Pull the cable until there is no slack and tighten the cable clamp bolt. Trim the inner sticking out of the clamp bolt, leaving about an inch, and fit a new end cap.

4 Unscrew (anti-clockwise) the barrel adjuster until any cable slack is removed. Then move on to the 'adjusting' section on page 139.

Setting the stops

1 A rear mech can sometimes push the chain further than necessary, and to prevent this there are two screw stops which physically limit the travel of the mech. To set the smallest sprocket stop, shift into the smallest sprocket (it's better to do this job at the same time as changing the cable, then cable tension doesn't have any effect) and screw in the adjusting screw – usually the top one of the two – until the chain starts to rub against the second sprocket. Then unscrew until the chain misses the second sprocket.

2 To adjust the top sprocket stop, shift into the largest sprocket (without the cable you can just push the mech across with your hand) and screw in the stop until the chain starts to get pushed off the largest sprocket. Then unscrew the stop slightly until the top jockey wheel is directly below the sprocket. When a chain over-shifts it can drop behind the largest sprocket and damage the spokes, or in severe cases the rear

REAR MECH: SETTING THE STOPS

REAR MECH: ADJUSTMENT AND INDEXING

mech can even be ripped off the frame. Some bike manufacturers fit small plastic discs between the wheel and sprocket to prevent this happening.

Adjustment and indexing

1 Indexed gear systems from Shimano and SunTour differ in the way they are set up. SunTour are better adjusted for shifting from smallest to the second sprocket, while Shimano are better set up for shifting from the second to third sprocket. Indexing adjustments are made by increasing or decreasing the cable tension using the barrel adjusters.

2 With a Shimano system, shift into the second sprocket (increase cable tension with the adjusters until you can shift from smallest to the second sprocket first of all) and screw the adjuster out until the chain just begins to rub on the third sprocket. Screw the adjuster back in a quarter of a turn and try the shifting. If the chain hesitates when shifting to a larger sprocket you need more cable tension and the barrel adjuster will have to be turned anti-clockwise. If it hesitates when dropping to a smaller cog, it means less tension is required and the adjuster should be turned clockwise. Adjust a small amount at a time and try the shifting between each adjustment. If you have a SunTour mech, the procedure is exactly the same except you begin the process with the chain on the smallest sprocket.

Brakes

The brakes are one of the most important components on a bike. I cannot stress too much how important it is to look after your braking system – your life may depend on it.

Inspect your brake cables regularly, preferably before every ride, and check for brake block or pad wear at least once every two weeks.

1 (The tyre has been removed to make the steps easier to see on page 140.) Remove the straddle wire quick release as if you were going to remove the wheel. Undo the cable clamp from the other brake arm and disconnect the

EMERGENCY REPAIRS

BENT CHAINRINGS

You know how it is, you bash your chainring on a rock and it's bent, aargh! But it's OK, it's almost certainly the big ring that hit and straightening it isn't too hard.
* Tighten the jaws of an adjustable spanner on the bent bit and use it as a lever to straighten it.
* No spanner? Bash it straight with a rock. You'll get it straight enough to take you home.

BUSTED REAR MECH

If your mech explodes, you can still ride home – just convert your bike to single speed. Here's how:
* Split the chain and remove it. Remove the rear mech. Replace the chain to give a gear you can ride home in (probably middle chainring and the rear sprocket which best suits the terrain ahead).
* Wrap the chain over the front chainring/rear sprocket you decide on and shorten it to a length which will fit over the gear you selected but is not so slack it comes off all the time.
* Join the chain and push it up the block with your fingers, turning a pedal slowly until the slack is taken up and you can ride the bike home.
* No chain tool? If you have a zip tie or two you can usually tie the rear mech to the chainstay and limp home that way.

cable. Next, unscrew (anti-clockwise) the brake boss bolts (5mm allen key).

2 Clean the brake bosses and the inside of the brake bush that fits over the boss. Re-install the brake on the boss and check that it rotates freely with no tight spots. Paint over-spray can be removed with fine emery paper sprayed with WD40 or similar. Grease the boss thoroughly after cleaning but don't get grease down the threads that run inside it.

3 Clean out the springs (run a rag between each coil) and then grease them to prevent corrosion. Do one cantilever at a time so as not to get the springs mixed up. If you do mix them up, then the wire of the spring should wind outwards and away from the wheel – opposite to that shown in the picture. The spring locates in a hole at the rear of the boss and, usually, there are three holes to choose from which allows you to adjust the spring tension. However, the middle hole is the best place to start.

4 Re-install the brake making sure that the spring engages in the recess inside the rear of the brake. Tighten the boss bolts tightly, but don't go over the top because it is easy to deform the boss and that will make the brake bind. Use a drop of thread-locking compound on all bolts connected with the braking system.

5 This shows by far the most common straddle wire system. The main brake cable runs through the left-hand side of the yoke and through the small diameter inner to the left-hand cantilever. A short link wire runs from the yoke to the right-hand cantilever and has a small line marked on it. When this marking is in line with the marking on the yoke, it is correctly set up.

6 Thread the cables into place and pull the main cable through on the left-hand cantilever until the two lines on the yoke line up, then tighten the cable clamp bolt.

7 Brake pad adjustment requires a 10mm spanner and, usually, a 5mm allen key, although some brakes use 6mm. The front of the block should be 2mm away from the rim, and the rear of the pad should be 3mm to 4mm away. This arrangement is what's called 'toe-in' alignment and

BRAKES

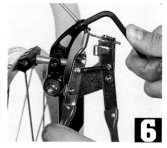

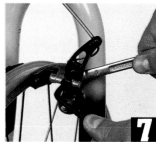

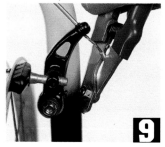

DIFFERENT BRAKE TYPES

Your brake system is possibly the most important component to keep in good working order – your life may depend on it.

prevents the brakes from squealing.

Toe-in works like this: when the front of the brake pad touches the wheel rim there is a tendency for the whole brake unit to flex slightly, which in effect pulls the rest of the block into contact with the rim (it happens anyway when you pull hard on the brake lever). If the front of the brake pad was further away from the rim than the back, then the front of the pad would be pushed away from the rim and the brake would vibrate and squeal.

8 The new style of brake uses a crosshead screw to adjust the spring tension. Tightening the screw increases the spring tension on the cantilever and pushes it away from the rim, while loosening brings it closer. A few pulls of the brake between adjustments and each pad should end up exactly the same distance from the wheel rim.

9 Finish the brake cable off neatly with an end cap. Leave about one to two inches of cable sticking out, then tuck it behind the small pin on the back of the brake so that it's out of the way.

Other brake types

Some brake systems use different spring tension devices and a more conventional straddle wire set-up.

A Spring tension on some brakes is adjusted by a nut at the rear of the brake. Loosen the boss bolt and turn the nut (usually with a 13mm cone spanner – Dia-Compe) until the desired tension is achieved. Some brakes have one either side and some have just the one side, the other being the more conventional spring in a hole at the rear of the boss. If they have nuts at both sides you must set both sides to the desired tension and then adjust one of them until they are balanced.

B A hanger and straddle wire like that pictured above used to be the most common system until Shimano stopped using it, but that doesn't mean it's no good. Most brakes work better if the angle between the straddle wire and cantilever (a line taken through the boss and where the cable attaches) is close to 90° when the pads touch the rim. A hanger like this is easy to adjust and you can experiment with angles.

more freedom, more excitement

W H A T   K I N D   O F   R I D E R   A R E   Y O U ,

W H A T   K I T   F I T S   Y O U R   S T Y L E ,

M T B   H E R O E S ,   X T R E M E   A N T I C S

We hope our book has given you the inspiration and information you need to really enjoy your mountain biking. If it has and you want more of the same, you'll find it in *MBUK* and *MTB Pro* every month.

Hello, it's me again. So what do you think? Is mountain biking the meaning of life or just something very like it? We've tried to give you the full flavour of the thing here, but now we're coming to the end of our book and we've hardly scratched the surface.

We've mainlined on the information you'll really need to get into the different facets of the game, because that's what a book like this is for, but the fact is, once you start talking about the bikes and the people who ride them, you can end up almost anywhere.

Take the machines themselves. If you really want to get the best out of them, you're led into an endless discussion of mechanics (fluid mechanics and elastomer tech too, now we've all got suspension). Scoots take in the (cliché alert) cutting edge of modern technology (sorry, but it's true).

The incredibly light, but amazingly strong materials we all take for

granted lead you even further: the composition characteristics, build qualities and ridability of some of those alloys is an endlessly fascinating subject.

It leads you swiftly through metallurgy and geology to global politics, when you discover that the countries which produce the vital alloying metals are almost all politically unstable, because they produce them.

This is strategic metal we're riding and that means Great Power manipulation, greed, exploitation and war.

Not, of course, that anyone goes to war and tears down mountains to build mountain bikes, we're just a by-product, but we do leave our mark on the earth's crust.

A very slight one, though. Mountain bikers are involved in the most ecologically sound, sustainable form of transport. We ought to be encouraged. And yet we're driven off the roads, squeezed off the railways and treated as a damn nuisance by every authority going. There's plenty more to say about that!

And there's plenty more to say too about access to the countryside, which is the root and branch of mountain biking, and the sad attitude of the dweeb minority of walkers; an attitude that hinders any form of co-operative solution.

Not helped by the fact that mountain bikers are the world's worst lobbying group, of course. There are huge numbers of us, we are mostly young, intelligent and articulate. But we hate committees and motions and rules and regulations.

The Roundheads are far too cavalier and the Cavaliers too far off the ground.

Which brings me back to the way people enjoy their riding.

Mountain bike culture

Having written what I think mountain biking is all about in Chapter 1, I've been sitting back watching the guys doing their stuff, and thinking how much all the different kinds of rider have got in common.

The Roundhead and Cavalier thing works, but it overlaps plenty.

I mean, for all the grinding endurance, painstaking preparation and rigorous planning that goes into assault mountain biking, there's something very cavalier about the way the Derek Purdys of this world look at a distant peak across the snow-bound mountains and decide to go for it.

Nothing more cavalier than Jase McRoy's five minute stack-or-glory downhill charge, but the training and preparation are as concentrated as anything a cross-country racer would put in, but in a different way.

Trick riders like to look very carefree and gung-ho, but behind that effortless mastery of gravity are hours and hours of doing the same move over and over again to perfect it.

Even cross-country racers can have a sense of humour – I mean, what could be funnier than Justin's sad bottom-out style? (And what a bottom!)

I guess mountain bikes are rather like musical instruments. A lot of people can play on them and they're all capable of making the same sound, but what comes out is dependent on each player's personality.

Look at the way you ride and the products you use to decide what sort of rider you are.

WHAT KIND OF RIDER ARE YOU?

How you ride says who you are and what kind of bike and kit you really need. And that's pretty important because it saves you wasting your money on stuff you're never really going to use. That's why we at *MBUK*, masters of crude generalisation, have split the mountain bike world into six distinct types, to help you decide.

Headbanger

Do you...
- Regularly go out to session a particular jump or trick spot?
- Crash hard at least once every time you go mountain biking?
- Regularly hit over 40mph off-road?
- Believe the meaning of life can be found in a Mint Sauce cartoon?

You're a big show-off. You want to jump, drop-off, hit things at speed and hammer downhill. You may be a downhill racer, but probably can't be arsed with rules and turning up on time. Very heavy on equipment. Spend loads for the best.

We suggest: Don't get carried away by lightweight kit – you need a heavy duty frame, gussets and all! Don't think you can get away without suspension forks, go for mega travel sorted elastomer forks. Make sure your bars are top quality and strong! Don't save money on the bars and stem. Monster rims too and big aggressive tyres.

Trailcat

Do you...
- Often lead the pack on new and unknown technical trails?
- Adapt instantly to new terrain?
- Wear a pair of MTB shades worth over £100?
- Believe the meaning of life can be found in a Mint Sauce cartoon?

The biggest headbanger of them all is Rob Warner, move over and let him rip.

You ride light and skilful, you're probably getting into suspension but not convinced you need it. You just love tough singletrack. You like to look the part. Spend loads on clothes, shades and trick bittery and why not?
We suggest: You try some really top quality ultra-rigid forks. They'll help you enjoy the super-light and wonderful framesets your riding style allows you to use. As for spending loads of dosh on lighter components, right down to the nuts and bolts – you're going to do that anyway. Just remember cheap and light simply don't go together.

Assault biker

Do you...
■ Frequently ride over 50 miles in a day (off-road)?
■ Camp out in open country overnight on tour?
■ Go on self-organised foreign MTB tours?
■ Believe the meaning of life can be found in a Mint Sauce cartoon?
You're a heavy duty tourist into mountains. You need functional kit that won't let you down. You don't take any notice of what the fashion plates think because you once had an aluminium frame bust on you in the Andes. Big challenges only should apply. Something of a retrogrouch.
We suggest: An easily repairable steel bike. Go for rigid forks and spend what suspension forks would have cost on better build quality and top quality components. Go for heavy duty expert-built wheels too. When you're miles from anywhere you depend on your bike staying in one piece while heavily laden. Stick to toe-clips and straps to go with a decent pair of walking/bike boots.

The panniers and wild, uncharted terrain give away the Assault biker.

Will Cogger is a typical Racehead, who lives to race and races to win.

Borasic budgeteer

Do you...
■ Ride a second-hand bike?
■ Strip and service your headset regularly?
■ Wear a pair of MTB shades worth less than £30?
■ Believe the meaning of life can be found in a Mint Sauce cartoon?
You're heavily into the sport but skint. You want the best gear but know you have to compromise for now. You want the best possible value for every bit of money. You compensate by being a mega fit animal.
We suggest: You get the bike with the best frame you can find for around £400 and upgrade as you can (see Chapter 2). It's going to weigh around 28lb, but you'll have a good workhorse. If £400 is too much, buy the best you can afford, have fun and learn your skills on it. Buy from a reputable dealer, though, and avoid anything that's really cheap and comes in a box.

Dirty weekender

Do you...
■ Take part in other sports to keep fit?
■ Ride off-road less than three times a week?
■ Go mountain biking with your family?
■ Believe the meaning of life can be found in a Mint Sauce cartoon?
No interest in racing, you want a great ride with friends/family. Commute to work to stay fit. A weekender because you've got a time-consuming job. Been through fashionable, big disposable income sports like wind-surfing. Own a flash bike but commute on a heap that won't get stolen.
We suggest: Forget the 'it's wasted on me' modesty and splurge out on the best, most innovative engineering going. Someone's got to encourage designers to keep producing stuff that costs megaquids at first but trickles down to the rest of us later, and it's going to be you. A beautiful machine is a pleasure to own even if you're a crap rider (I speak from experience).

Racehead

Do you...
■ Stick to specific race training programmes?
■ Belong to a club or team?
■ Plan to compete in one of the major series this season?
■ Believe the meaning of life can be found in a Mint Sauce cartoon?
You live to race and race to win. Probably do XC at expert level. You train a ridiculous amount, are heavily into energy drinks, turbo trainers, diet, and the lightest, best equipment. Racing is your social life. Your partner doesn't understand you. Totally hooked.
We suggest: Get a road bike. Seriously. You're going to have to put in plenty of road miles to get to the level of fitness you want and a road bike will get the max out of your body. You can't handle off-road terrain efficiently on road bike geometry, but your race bike will be as close to it as you can get. Get the feel of max efficiency and check out Chapter 6.

MTB ICONS

As with all underground cultures, lots of names fly around in mountain bike conversations and they usually stand for more than just the person. It's kind of useful to know who's who.

US RIDERS
Tomes (John Tomac)
Tomac can ride downhill and cross-country and win. He's the greatest all round rider with an aggressive riding style that shouts: 'Rebel!' The real Tomes is a quiet, religious, hunting shooting and fishing country boy and family man. But a rebel to the core.

Nedly (Ned Overend)
Deadly Nedly is guts on wheels. He just keeps on coming. Now 40, he's still feared at world class level. Nothing showy or loud about Ned, he's so modest it's painful. But when the chips are down Ned the Shred just won't quit. Sweet bike handler.

Greg Herbold, a star on the world circuit.

Hairball (Greg Herbold)
When the roadie cross-country clan had mountain biking by the short liners, the wild downhill image went way out. But Hairball didn't buy it. Ultra-mad brains-out downhill attitude, combined with extreme machines and cool-a-mundo clobber. A star.

No Way (Hans Rey)
Actually German Swiss, but an adopted Yank, Hans is just the trickiest of trick riders. If it's spectacularly dangerous, he's done it – with a posse of cameras along to prove it. It's high octane glam, but Hans will stand in the rain signing autographs till the last young fan's gone home.

Cully (Dave Cullinan)
World Champ downhiller, then he had a massive heart attack. One artificial heart valve later Dave was back, but they wouldn't let him ride. So he had human heart valves installed and was back racing downhill for the 1985 season. *'Downhilling is my life,'* says Dave.

Dave Cullinan after a fast downhill run. (Check out that double pinch flat... Hardcore!)

Modelling the latest mountain bike fashion gear, John Tomac and Greg Herbold in lederhosen.

The daddy of them all, Ned Overend, has been racing mountain bikes for ever; he's 40 and still winning.

How does he do that? Hans 'No Way' Rey displays the sort of riding that has made him famous the world over.

UK RIDERS
Tim Gould

He came from cyclo-cross with his sideburns and silly bunch-of-bananas roadie hat and hammered the mountain bikers into the ground on a steel bedstead. He was the first Roundhead but no one resented Tim. Won the uphill at the first World Championships. Icon of individualism.

Top Boy (Rob Warner)

Rebellion in motion. Rob hurtled into the *MBUK* team from motorbike trials and took on the world, leaving a trail of bent bikes and enraged sponsors in his wake. Completely fearless, utterly outrageous, completely focused. The Yanks call him 'the Mad Axeman'. Awesome and then some.

Racin' Jasin' (Jason McRoy)

Commitment incarnate. Determined to be a world class downhiller, Jase did well in Europe with Team *MBUK*, but wanted more. Took redundancy, hocked everything and took on the Yanks at home. Second in the Eliminator, now with Team Specialized.

Rob Warner only rides one way – ATTACK!

David Baker

Hit mountain biking along with Tim Gould, but people did resent David. He was too much a roadie, and too mindful of roadie team ethics where a rider may not sneeze without permission. National Champion, but it took an article on gardening in *MBUK* to reveal he does have a dry sense of humour.

Jez Hot Pie (Jez Avery)

Mega bunny-hopper and crazed trick rider, Jez is a natural crowd pleaser. If this was America he'd be a sponsored hero. The Avery speciality is the wheelie with the front wheel flipped out and the Switzerland Squeaker – balanced on the front with no back wheel. Easy.

Mr Crud (Pete Tomkins)

Also known as Captain Sensible, long time crazed downhiller Pete Tomkins was the man who had the nerve to turn a bit of plastic into the Crud Catcher. Made Dave's Chain Device and the Crud Guard. Pete just makes things he himself needs including, incidentally, lots of money.

When it comes to downhilling, no one looks quite as stylish as Racin' Jason McRoy.

Jez Avery is trickmeister supreme, the UK's answer to Hans Rey when it comes to amazing stunts.

Always a contender for cross-country gold, Tim Gould, the UK's original racing hero.

King of the widget is Mr Crud, aka Pete Tomkins (above). David Baker (overleaf) is always in the hunt for medals.

MBUK JOURNOS

Mountain Biking UK was the first British mountain bike magazine, and the people who work on it have influenced the scene quite a bit.

People like:

Justin Loretz

Justin has been a reader of *MBUK* since issue 1. He started as understudy to ex Dep Ed John Stevenson before taking over the helm in the *MBUK* office. Double Blue Peter badge winner and all round stunt type person, Justin recently lived out another of his burning ambitions by jumping his bike through a ring of fire.

Brant Richards

Engineer, innovator and classy technical rider, Brant (named after a mountaineering climb in Wales) actually made bar ends and crud catchers as a teenager, but never went into production. Preferred partying, DJing, organising slaloms and overseeing the technical side of *MBUK*. Can be a stroppy northern git.

Rugged and Windswept (Steve Worland)

MBUK's Test Editor, Steve's been around bikes most of his life, original member of the Fisher team and now one of the Vets from Hell. He's tested so many bikes over the years he has a better grasp of the market than most manufacturers and is impervious to fashion. Mr value for money.

The Rain Maker (Steve Behr)

MBUK's ace lensman, Steve is one of the few photographers who can make the camera tell the truth. The Behr technique shows you how steep the vert was, how fast the action was – you can almost hear the tyres humming. He's so good, rain clouds follow him everywhere to see how he does it.

Jo Burt

Innocent art student Jo Burt carelessly scrawled a cartoon of a sheep on a mountain bike one day and was instantly trapped! Ever since, he has shared his life with a thin-legged megalomaniac ovine, drunk with fame. It's amazing how well he puts up with it really.

Jo Burt, a man with a legal relationship with a sheep.

Looking for yet another Blue Peter badge, Justin the boy and his toy jump for joy.

Stroppy northern DJ Brant Richards tries hard to be meaningful in the facial hair department.

Steve Worland, *MBUK*'s bike test editor (and that's a caterpillar not a bogey).

Steve Behr is the lens of *MBUK*. Nothing is too much for the ultimate image.

BIKE ANTICS

Riding bikes down mountains was a pretty crazy idea to start with and ever since riders have been coming up with waz ideas and bringing them to *MBUK*. Most of which fall into the 'don't do this at home' category.

Riding the sea-bed

Clive and Julian said that they wanted to ride to France under the English Channel. They were joking, of course, but these two highly trained and generally sensible divers were deadly serious about attempting to ride their bikes underwater. And they did, riding into the sea and along the bottom, getting seriously lost at record downhill speeds of 2mph. Sea water doesn't do great things for your bike and bits, though.

75ft jump

In 1989 World Windsurf Champion Dave Perks felt like riding off a 75ft cliff into the sea. It was just one more ridiculously dangerous challenge for Dave, but it didn't come that easy. He climbed the cliff first, to get a psychological grip of the height, but once up there nerves set in. He needed a ten yard run-up to be sure of getting clear of the cliff and that was the trouble. He kept bottling out.

And then he didn't! Aaaarrgh!

MBUK takes you to the places other bike mags just can't reach – like the bottom of the ocean (below).
Opposite – Anyone for cliff diving? Dave Perks had to overcome a distinct attack of the heebie geebies before launching off.

Balloonatics

Sometimes *MBUK* is just a excuse to do something very silly. Like riding with a propane burner on your back and taking off under a hot air balloon. Then Deputy Editor, John Stevenson, said he was trying to beat the bunny-hop record, but really he was after a free flight! His balloon was tethered, though. Free flight is for qualified aeronauts only.

Riding the clouds

In 1990, feeling *MBUK* was becoming too sensible, Dave Morris decided to ride his bike out of the back of a Skyvan at 7000ft, beating the bunny-hop record by rather more than a mile. Professional skydiver Dave had spent around 36 hours in freefall – experienced or what! Cool too. Holding the front wheel straight between his toes, he made a perfect landing. Tried to ride away but the wind caught the chute and pulled him over.

Drop that chicken!

Tired of criticism by dweeb walkers, *MBUK* printed a list of things readers simply should not do on their bikes: Dog hopping, Rambler slalom, Golf green jumping, and so on – all the things angry ramblers try to pretend

mountain bikers get up to. Charging through groups of picnickers and scooping the food from their plates was considered particularly bad form.

MAGAZINES WITH ATTITUDE

MBUK is the best-selling British MTB magazine and we hope this book has given you an inkling of why that might be. It's for adrenalin-lovers and guys who ride for the hell of it, backed up by the toughest, most objective technical experts and testers in the biz. Then there's *MTB Pro*, for those who take their riding just a tad more seriously. They don't ride underwater in *Pro*, they're trying to get good enough to ride on it!

In this book we've given you the essential info and attitude that everyone needs to have on hand. The mags take it from there, telling you what's new, what's happening, with proper emphasis on the fun and foolishness which is the why of it all.

SEE YOU THERE!

Above – 'It can't be done!' Oh yes it can, it's *MBUK*.
Right – How to cool off after all that red hot action.

Opposite – Balloon biking upset a few traditionalists, but there's nothing traditional about *MBUK*.

GLOSSARY

A

Aheadset
The trade name of a newer design of headset, which uses an unthreaded steerer tube. The stem clamps on externally (see Expander wedge)

Allen key
Hexagonal drive bar, in various sizes, that fits into the head of an allen bolt. Most bikes use allen bolts

Alloy
Bicycle trade word for aluminium alloy, derived from the 'al' of aluminium. Not strictly the proper meaning of the word

Aluminium
A metal used in the production of bike frames and components. Very light and can be built into very rigid frames if used in an oversize format

Anodising
Treatment process that colours or hardens the surface of aluminium

ANSI
A US standards testing organisation that, for our purposes, sets a helmet standard

B

Bar ends
Bolt-on extensions to your handlebars that give you extra and more powerful positions to climb or cruise with

Bearings
The round balls that rotate on bearing surfaces inside your hubs and bottom brackets

Bolt circle diameter (BCD)
The diameter of the circle drawn through the centre of the chainring bolts. Important to know when ordering replacements

Boss
A frame fitting that's welded directly to the frame tubes

Bottom bracket
The bearing that the cranks spin on, held in the bottom bracket shell

Brazing
A frame construction technique using brass to join tubes together

Bunny hop
Lifting the bike clear of the ground by pulling up on the bars and pedals

Butting
A metal component that has the wall thickness or section increased in a step is said to be butted

C

Cadence
The rate (in revs/sec) at which you pedal

Cantilevers
The brakes that are typically fitted to all mountain bikes. They run on bosses welded to the forks or rear stays

Cartridge bearings
A sealed bearing unit that pops into a shell, containing the bearing surfaces, ball bearings, grease and dirt seals

Chainrings
The (usually three) cogs that are fitted to the chainset. They increase in size from the inner to the outer

Chainset
The complete assembly of crank, chainrings and bottom bracket

Chainstays
The frame tubes that run from the bottom bracket shell to the rear dropout

Chainsuck
When the chainring refuses to let go of the chain, the chain gets sucked between the chainset and chainstay, usually causing damage

Chromoly
A high strength steel alloy used in bicycle frame construction

Cleat
A hardened metal plate that clips into a clipless pedal's mechanism, locking the shoe to it

Crank
The metal arms that run from the pedal to the bottom bracket axle

Crank extractor
Specialist tool for removing crank arms

Crud Catcher
Plastic clip-on front mudguard that's practically essential for UK riding conditions

D

Damping
A speed sensitive system which uses oil to control the movement of a suspension system

Derailleur
The mechanism that pushes the chain across the sprockets or chainwheels when a shift lever is moved

Disc brake
A braking system that works on a disc mounted to the hub, rather than working on the rim

Dish
The amount a wheel is offset on the hub. A rear wheel is dished to give room for the sprockets

Double butted
A tube that has greater wall thickness at both ends than in the middle section is double butted

Down tube
The frame tube that runs from the bottom of the head tube to the bottom bracket

Dropout
The plate welded to the frame or forks, where the wheels locate into the frame

Elastomers
Synthetic rubbers that have elastic properties. Used in suspension forks as a spring and damping medium

Endo
A trick involving tripping your bike forwards on its front wheel by locking the front wheel

Expander wedge
Used to jam the traditional stem inside the steerer tube of the fork (see Aheadset)

First
The lowest gear, also referred to as the granny gear

Flange
The part of the hub the spokes thread through

Fork
The part of the bike that holds the front wheel, and turns to allow steering

Frame
The main skeleton of the bike, consisting of down tube, top tube, head tube, seat tube, chainstays, seat stays and bottom bracket shell

Freewheel
Cunningly designed hub that lets the

wheel go on turning when you stop pedalling. Without it the popularity of the bicycle would be nil. The opposite is the fixed wheel, used by a certain type of obsessed cyclist. (See retrogrouch)

Front mech
The gear mechanism that shifts the chain across the chainwheels

Gear ratio
A method of determining the gearing of the bike, measured in effective wheel diameter (gear inches)

Gore-tex
A waterproof fabric that breathes. Used to make the best quality cycling and outdoor clothing

Granny ring
The smallest chainring

Gripshift
A type of gear changing system relying on twist-grip activation

Groupset
The core of the bike's components: gears, brakes, hubs, bearings, cranks, headset

Handlebar
The part of the bike that your grips, shifters and levers mount to

Head tube
The short tube that runs from the top of the forks to the bottom of the stem. Contains the headset

Headset
The bearing in which the fork steerer tube rotates, contained in the headtube

Hub
The unit that holds the bearings and supports the spokes at the centre of the wheel

Hyperglide
Brand name of Shimano rear gear sprockets which have profiled teeth and special 'shift ramps' for easier shifting under load

Indexing
Gears which click from position to position, making selecting the right one easy

Jockey wheels
The two small wheels which guide the chain in the rear derailleur

Knobblies
Aggressive tyres for true off-road use

Lacing
The process or type of spoking pattern used on wheels

Lube
Anything from oil to heavy duty grease. Dry lubes evaporate leaving a dry film (usually based on teflon). Wet lubes remain wet to the touch. Dry lubes are good for dusty conditions because they don't pick up dirt; wet lubes protect better in wet conditions

Lycra
Stretch fabric that makes you look fatter than you really are

Nipple
Small brass or alloy threaded adjuster that fixes the spokes to the rim

Nylock
A nut with a nylon insert which the bolt thread cuts into, designed to stop the nut working loose. Very useful for fixing pannier racks and so on

Oversize
Anything larger than normal. Most mountain bikes now have oversize tubing. It just means it's a bigger diameter than the first mountain bike tubing used

Presta
The thin valve, used more commonly on racing bikes, and the choice for some off-road riders. (See Schrader)

Quick release (QR)
A mechanism that allows quick and easy tightening, usually of the wheel hub/axle assembly and the seatpost clamp

Rapidfire
A type of shifter, made by Shimano, which operates with two levers, one moving the chain to a smaller sprocket or chainring, and the other moving it to a larger sprocket

Rear mech
The gear mechanism that moves the

chain across the rear sprockets. AKA the rear derailleur

Retrogrouch
One who believes (or pretends to believe) that new advanced equipment is hyped-up, expensive and unnecessary. Holds that the old equipment was just as good. In mountain biking the retrogrouch is sadly wrong

Rim
The metal hoop of the wheel that the tyre runs on

Schrader
The type of valve found on cars and some mountain bikes

Seal
Any part intended to stop muck getting into the internals of something delicate, like a bearing

Seatstays
The frame tubes that run from where the seatpost enters the frame to the rear dropouts

Seat tube
The tube that holds the seatpost and runs down to the bottom bracket

Seatpost
The tube that is clamped in the frame and supports the saddle

Shifters
The levers on the handlebars that allow you to change gear

Shimano
The Japanese component manufacturer which has almost total market dominance on production bikes. Makes good, reliable equipment

Sidewall
The side of a tyre. The bit without tread

Slider
The moving part of a suspension fork leg

SPD
The original mountain bike clipless pedal system, made by Shimano. Affectionately known as SPuDs

Spoke key
Tool which turns spoke nipples and adjusts spoke tension. A wheel wrecker in the wrong hands

Spokes
The thin metal wires that run from the hub to the rim

Sprockets
The cogs at the rear of the bike that are driven by the chain

Stanchion
The fixed part of a suspension fork leg

Steerer tube
The tube that runs inside the head tube, locating the headset and supporting the front fork

Stem
The welded tube assemby that connects the handlebar to the front fork

Thumbshifters
The original gearshift levers, pushed with the thumb. Popular with some riders but harder and harder to get

TIG welding
The frame building technique that uses heat from pulses of electricity to join tubes. Used extensively on production bikes and US custom frames

Titanium
The oft-hailed wonder metal of the modern age. Very expensive, light and strong

Top tube
The horizontal frame tube that runs from the top of the head tube to the top of the seat tube

Truing
The process of straightening a wheel by adjusting the tension of the spokes

Wheelbase
The distance between the front and rear axles

RECOMMENDED READING

First Aid On Mountains, Dr Steve Bollen, British Mountaineering Council £1 (available from most outdoor shops or BMC at 177-179, Burton Road, West Didsbury, Manchester M20 2BB ☎ 0161 445 4747

Advanced Mountain Biking, Derek Purdy, Springfield Books £14.95

Mountain Bike Racing, Tim Gould and Simon Burney, Springfield Books £12.95

The Heart Rate Monitor Book, Sally Edwards, distributed by Leisure Systems International £8.99

Grime Time, Paul Smith, Future Books £11.99

INDEX

Mountain biking, it's all about having fun in the dirt.